MAIN STREET

Bob Dylan's Minnesota

Toby Thompson

Bonus Track: Interview with the Author

Revised Edition

University of Minnesota Press
Minneapolis
London

Selections from the *Village Voice* reprinted by permission of the *Village Voice;* copyright 1969 by The Village Voice, Inc.

Selections from the San Francisco *Chronicle* reprinted by permission of the San Francisco *Chronicle;* copyright 1969 by the San Francisco *Chronicle.*

"Hey Hey Woody Guthrie I Wrote You a Song" from *US 2* reprinted by permission of Bantam Books, Inc.; copyright 1969 by Bantam Books, Inc.

"An Interview with the Author" was originally published in *The Bridge* 21 (Spring 2005); reprinted by permission of Terry Kelly and *The Bridge.*

Photographs by Toby Thompson

Copyright 1971 by Toby Thompson

Preface to the New Edition copyright 2008 by Toby Thompson

Originally published in hardcover by Coward-McCann & Geoghegan, Inc.

First University of Minnesota Press edition, 2008

Published by the University of Minnesota Press
111 Third Avenue South, Suite 290
Minneapolis, MN 55401-2520
http://www.upress.umn.edu

Library of Congress Cataloging-in-Publication Data

Thompson, Toby.
  Positively Main Street : Bob Dylan's Minnesota / Toby Thompson. — 1st University of Minnesota Press ed.
      p.   cm.
  ISBN 978-0-8166-5445-1 (pb : alk. paper)
  1. Dylan, Bob, 1941–   Childhood and youth.   2. Dylan, Bob, 1941– Homes and haunts—Minnesota.   I. Title.
  ML420.D98T52   2008
  782.42164092—dc22
  [B]   2008008167

Printed in the United States of America on acid-free paper

The University of Minnesota is an equal-opportunity educator and employer.

15 14 13 12 11 10 09 08   10 9 8 7 6 5 4 3 2 1

POSITIVELY MAIN STREET

POSITIVELY

*That boy ... this fellow, Toby ...
has got some lessons to learn.*

—Bob Dylan, *Rolling Stone,*
November 29, 1969

To the memory of my parents:
Charles and Elizabeth Thompson

CONTENTS

PREFACE TO THE NEW EDITION

It started when the wiry fan handed me a Highway 61 bumper sticker. He was nervous, distracted, but when he looked at my name tag he focused and dug into his tote bag. "Here," he said. "Take this." The sticker was four inches square and white on black, but beneath it was a rare hardcover copy of *Positively Main Street*, published in 1971. "Where did you get that?" I asked. "Sign the title page," he said.

We stood in a reception area of Minneapolis's fantastic and futuristic Weisman Art Museum in 2007, on the first day of a three-day symposium titled "Highway 61 Revisited: Dylan's Road from Minnesota to the World." Surrounding us near the Frank Gehry–designed gallery overlooking the Mississippi River were the heavies of what has come to be known as Dylan Studies: Christopher Ricks, Greil Marcus, Michael Gray, Dave Marsh, Dave Engel, and the musicians Bobby Vee, "Spider" John Koerner, and Tony "Little Sun" Glover, former Dylan sidekicks, plus the post-Beat poet Anne Waldman and about sixty-five other participants in what, no doubt, was the largest Dylan conference ever assembled.

The scholars sat at tables in the Weisman's Shepherd Room, signing and selling their books. *Positively Main Street* had been out of print since 1977, so I had no seat but as I stood in the museum people jabbed hardcover and paperback copies of American and British editions at me. I was flabbergasted. Though I had never stopped receiving mail about the book, this was unexpected. People had lugged copies from as far away as Japan.

The heavies all seemed to have read it; likewise had their fans. But as the reception progressed, I felt a sense of dislocation. *Positively Main Street* had been the first biography to attempt an examination of Dylan's life in Minnesota. In its wake, at least four hundred Dylan titles have been published. I continued to write books and magazine articles on various topics. Though I had taught nonfiction writing at Penn State since 1985, I did not consider myself an academic—I was too much a journalist for that. Yet here I was on a "Rolling Tenure Review," in *Nation* critic Richard Goldstein's phrase, at a conference with a presentation scheduled about a world (both Dylan's and mine) so faraway that I felt like Moondog, the Greenwich Village eccentric who costumed himself like a Viking to hawk his poetry.

In the adjacent auditorium, a musician with guitar and harmonica barked the rusty classics, while an atticful of Dylan memorabilia waited in the Weisman's galleries: the traveling exhibition "Bob Dylan's American Journey, 1956–1966," augmented for its Minneapolis showing with numerous pieces from Dylan's Hibbing boyhood and stint at the University of Minnesota. In 1968, during the first of my two trips to Minnesota's North Country, I saw much of this in situ: artifacts from the Zimmerman residence, from Hibbing High, and from Echo Helstrom, Dylan's high school sweetheart and inspiration for "Girl from the North Country." I toured Dinkytown, Minneapolis's boho quarter, when the Ten O'Clock Scholar offered folk music, and I interviewed Dylan's brother in the chilly canyons of downtown.

Dylan was in seclusion then, a Garboesque figure who, absent since his motorcycle accident in 1966, had Hulked to superhero proportions. He was sage, oracle, and apocalyptic poet rolled into one. I was a beginning writer, having just finished grad school in English literature but intrigued by a highly personal brand of reporting called New Journalism. That summer of '68, Tom Wolfe (New Journalism's most celebrated practitioner) published, on the same day, two books, one of which was *The Electric Kool-Aid Acid Test,* his classic about Ken Kesey and the Merry Pranksters. Tired of fiction and its veiled introspection, I hoped to find a project that might get me out of my study and onto the American road. Because America was the story. Even then, at twenty-three, I sensed that my generation's "revolutionary" consciousness couldn't understand what it was until it understood where it had been (the Beatles were singing, "Get back to where you once belonged"). So I envisioned a heartland piece about the Main Street roots of the counterculture's hippest icon. This book (and the six-part *Village Voice* article that preceded it) is the culmination of that vision and a compendium of what I found.

Once I began to write, I realized celebrity was key—not just from the star's side but the fan's, too. The complicity in hero worship is perilous to both. It's part of what Christopher Lasch dubbed "the culture of narcissism." So I chose to tell Dylan's and my stories concurrently. (Henry James's biographer Leon Edel noted in *Writing Lives:* "The relation of the biographer to his subject is the very core of the biographical enterprise.") Some readers were troubled by this tack, but William Kennedy, the Pulitzer Prize–winning author of *Ironweed* and other novels, understood it and wrote for *Look* magazine the best review *Positively Main Street* received: "A first rate novelistic account of Thompson's own psyche . . . a new look at young Dylan, done with kindness, enthusiasm, and superb language." He reviewed it in tandem with Richard Brautigan's novel *The Abortion,* and I couldn't have asked for better company.

Brautigan loved *Positively Main Street,* by the way, and years later, when we became friends, he told me he kept a copy by his bedside. Why, I'm not sure. Like Dylan, he had grown up in remote towns and knew their potential for angst. He knew Dylan, too. In his cups, Richard more than once threatened to phone him to ask what he thought of my book. I'm glad he didn't. Over the years I've heard variously from Dylan's intimates that he liked it so well he kept it on his desk, or, conversely, that he was "concerned" about its contents, or, moderately, that characters like Echo "came off pretty good in the book." I conclude this new edition by reprinting a long interview (published in the British magazine *The Bridge* in 2005) that speaks much of my relationship to Dylan.

In his *Rolling Stone* interview with Jann Wenner in 1969, Dylan said the best thing he could have about the six-part *Village Voice* article that became *Positively Main Street:* "I wouldn't have read it if I thought he was using me to write his story...I can see through this writer's aims." And "if they want to spend six or seven issues writing about me (laughs)...as long as they get it right, you know, as long as they get it in there, I can't complain." But he had reservations about my having mentioned his father's death: "I didn't dig him talking about my father and using his name. Now that's the only thing about the article I didn't dig. But that boy has got some lessons to learn."

He later told a biographer, Anthony Scaduto: "That thing about my father, I was going to ask Wenner to cut that...because it wasn't what I really felt." But I did have lessons to learn. The second half of *Positively Main Street* examines them in a deliberately memoiristic style. Marginally, *Positively Main Street*, finished in late 1969, anticipated the '70s frenzies of first-person journalism and the '90s memoir craze. As Richard Goldstein wrote in the final section of the original book, "Taking a biography and turning it into a postcard from home, letting the beams and girders in your work show, imposing your own private myth upon a larger public one—that's some of what New Journalism is about." *Positively Main Street* was "hi-octane prose, open-road stuff like Mailer hitch-hiking between points. But cagy the way Tom Wolfe is cagy, and so damned charming (though I can't think of a contemporary charmer)."

So here I was at the Weisman, signing books, thinking about getting *Positively Main Street* back into print, *planning* to get it into print, while wondering what sort of presentation I might give. Symposium calendars promised I would speak about "Echo and Beatty," Dylan's girlfriend and mother, whom I had interviewed in 1968 and 1969. But I still wasn't certain of the context. What I wished to explain was that a biographer must put oneself in one's hero's shoes, and if that meant flirting with his ex-flame and braving the wrath of a disapproving mother, so be it. How one *felt* in one's hero's shoes was the fiercest indicator of what one's hero might have felt. Facing Echo, I felt exciting, talented, and sexy; facing Beatty, I felt childish, guilty, and wrong. In Hibbing, I felt the town's, the region's, isolation, along with my passion to connect; in Dinkytown, I felt the torpor of its dying scene.

The latter had revitalized since my visit in 1968. After the Weisman's reception, I hiked through an imposing University of Minnesota campus to Fourteenth Avenue Southeast, Dinkytown's main drag. It was warm for March, and couples lingered at sidewalk café tables or darted into coffee shops and bookstores. An upscale bohemianism was evident. I walked to the corner of Fourth Street, where the Ten O'Clock Scholar had been. Dylan started as a folk singer there. Its space was now the parking lot for a video outlet. I backtracked to Gray's Drugstore, above which Dylan had lived in 1960 and at whose counter, in 1969, I'd sipped a chocolate soda while scribbling notes. The space in 2007 was a trendy restaurant. One could sit in its dining room and, if in the know, stare through an overhead gallery at the door to Dylan's room. The following night I would dine here with Colleen Sheehy, the symposium's chair, and participants with ties to Hibbing, including Mary Feidt, director of the documentary *Tangled Up in Bob;* Bill Pagel, who runs the Dylan website www.boblinks.org and owns twelve original copies of *Positively Main Street;* and Bob and Linda Hocking, proprietors of Zimmy's, Hibbing's Dylan-themed restaurant and bar. We would note with irony that we, participants in a Bob Dylan conference, were partying grandly in the building where Bob, forty-seven years past, had cooked on a hot plate and used the toilet down the hall.

I ordered and thought about what I might do for my presentation. Near here, on a spring night in '69, I collected Echo from her Minneapolis apartment and we drove up Highway 65 toward Hibbing. We parked at Big Sandy Lake, studied the moon, drank glove-compartment Scotch, then danced until closing at Hibbing's Garden Lounge. Perhaps I would read that chapter. Anne Waldman had paced her way through a manic essay on Dylan's association with the Beats; afterward when we spoke she advised, for my performance, to "get out from behind that podium." That's what I would do: skip the academics and go with the Kerouac road-warrior shtick. Pacing wildly, I would read a scene from *Positively Main Street* that featured Echo, then retreat to the lectern for a more sober encounter with Beatty, from my comeuppance chapter. "You're up here with that Echo," she had said.

That's right, I thought. And I miss her. So I paid my bill and walked toward Fourth Street, where Dylan, Echo, and I had once been young.

ACKNOWLEDGMENTS

For this new edition, thanks to Terry Winch for suggesting its republication to editors at the University of Minnesota Press; to Ellen Levine of Trident Media for closing the deal; to Ken McCullough, Sandy Rock, Rick Winking, and William Crawford Woods for friendship and criticism; to Richard Goldstein for permitting the reprint of his "Postgush" to the 1971 edition; to Terry Kelly, for giving permission to reprint his interview with me for *The Bridge;* and to Pieter Martin at the University of Minnesota Press for his enthusiasm and smarts in editing this book.

For the original *Positively Main Street,* thanks to John Holland for his early suggestions and encouragement; to Diane Fisher for editing the *Voice* series; to Scott Wright for a desk in the Morris House; to Linn Barnes for blues accompaniment; to Jack Odell for philosophical dialogue; to Damon Taylor for songs and camaraderie; and to all participants from Minneapolis and Hibbing, especially Echo Star Helstrom, without whose help both editions would have suffered irreparably.

Special thanks to my sweetheart, Belinda Winslow. Her support in this endeavor and all others means so much.

INTROGUSH

If you're* really *a Dylan buff, I mean tuned right into the stereo microgrooves of his soul, you'll get a kick out of this. I just finished speaking with the "Girl from the North Country." Right, the very same chick Bob wrote the song about. Her name's Echo and she has long, Swedish blond hair that rolls and flows, and she's a friend of mine.

That's not all either. Not by a long shot. I can't imagine you missed the six articles I had last spring in the *Village Voice* about Bob's hometown, plus the follow-up piece for Richard Goldstein in *US*, but I'll mention them anyway just in case you did and try to run down a little of what's been happening to me since. Well, this book for openers. It's already been sold and I'm living off of the money they gave me to get this manuscript out. As you can see, I'm only on the first page. But don't get turned off, the action'll pick up. It's just that I spend a lot of time these days doing other things—talking on the phone long distance—and answering letters. You should *see* the letters. I got one last week from a lady in Queens who had heard about my series in the *Voice* and wanted copies for her seventy-one-year-old mother who is a Dylan freak and can't go out . . . and the week before that, the sweetest little note from a high school girl in Flushing who needed information on Bob for a term paper she was writing . . . and five weeks back a card from a fellow who wanted Bob's telephone number so he could invite him to a one-man art show being held in his honor . . . I try to answer all my mail as honestly as I can, but there're some people I just can't help. First off, I've never *met* Bob, let alone know his phone number; I'm like a whole lot of the rest of you in that respect. Oh, I suppose I'll run into him someday. You simply don't write seven articles and a book about a person who's still alive without meeting him. Or do you? In any case, that doesn't matter here. What we're concerned with is the past; and not exclusively Bob Dylan's. An entire generational pudding should ooze through your skull if I play my cards right—laced with remembrances, true and false. Try to keep that in mind. And watch the pitfalls, there's a herd of responsibilities milling about here. Again, more than are due just Bob Dylan. He gets to be the star, *la petite madeleine* as it were, but that little seventy-one-year-old lady in Queens and people all over the place who need to know, they're equally as important, culpable . . . and alive! That's really it right there, that's the point, underline it—*Bob Dylan is alive!* To be quite frank, that's something I hadn't realized until recently . . . that Bob Dylan is an actual, fleshy person with a hometown and friends who remember him and a house where he grew up. And a wife and kids now. He breathes our air, poisons it, and probably watches the same TV shows. You know he listens to much of the same music. So . . . here's a book about Bob Dylan's, no, Bobby *Zimmerman's* past, that's really concerned with a good deal more. What book isn't? I don't know. My phone's ringing, but I'm going to take it off the hook and disregard the mailman for a while, and maybe I'll be able to get this thing started. I think it might be worth your while to bear with me . . . I know a lot of great stories.

FIRST TRIP

ONE GUSH: *Humdrum Star Dumb, Silver Sagedom*

If the moon had been full, my horoscope hesitant, a solstice near, or the temperature in flux, I might have been prepared. But as it stands, all I can pinpoint as "out of the ordinary" on the afternoon in question was that I'd stopped by a porno newsstand. It was hot, I remember, the pavement was sweating. Washington's humidity hadn't let up since early June, and the candy wrappers, Dixie cups, and cigar butts in the street were spewing up an ultra-natural phew. Washington was still a swamp; that hadn't changed. Nor was it specifically my dalliance among the flowers of pornography that gave my day significance. I'm not characteristically a smut aficionado—the pleasures of *Spanky: The Magazine with the Belt in the Back, Stud,* and other such journals afford me few moments of glee; but the marketplace of pornography itself, the cavelike shops, faces of those who buy and sell . . . that fascinates me. I can spend hours.

There is invariably a withered old man behind the cash register. He sits in his chair watching portable television or listens to the ball game on a transistor radio cupped to his ear. He always appears upset when his customers approach to pay. He sounds them right-eously before wrapping their purchases in shiny brown paper sacks. Very few people can look him in the eye.

This shop isn't exactly special, but it does have a flair that only one or two such newsstands I've patronized are capable of matching. I suppose variety's the touchstone. That old man behind the register knows his market; he sells the hardcore stuff, sure, and plenty of it—but that's not his limit. He handles movie mags, newspapers, comic books, true romance slicks, and outdoorsman sagas as well. He's got too much savvy to specialize. He knows his public. You have to admire him. And the way he has everything bunched together in one room, you get a chance to see many different types of people passing through—businessmen, schoolgirls, tiny kids, mothers, nurses, pervertos, laundromat attendants, diplomats... it's very hard to tell who's buying what. Or what *is* what.

Take the former Mrs. J. F. K. for example: She's spread out all over the store. There's a rack of movie magazines to the left of the cash register, flaunting headlines like JACKIE DINES AT SUCH-AND-SUCH IN THE COMPANY OF THE ARCHDUKE SO-AND-SO, or DOES SCORPIO HOLD THE KEY TO JACKIE'S HEART? And overhead there's an entire fashion section devoted to her wardrobe. *Time* discloses the exact amount she spent last year on clothes, while *Business Week* or the like predicts what effect her marriage to Onassis will have on a shaky Greek economy. The true-confessions shelves bulge with provocatively packaged Jackie-dirt. Even girls on the covers of lesbo slicks sport Jackie-inspired bouffant hairdos and sensitively pasteled lips.

Our First Lady, America's only Marquesa. Look what we've done to you! Prepubescent girls pore over your Caesarean scars, while businessmen calculate their futures on reports of your charge accounts; teen-age housewives court improbable dreams of menopausal fulfillment between the lines of your grandeur, while bathroom ghouls the world over *spurt spout splush* their cancered horniness into your face, that face!... Look what you've done to *us!*

Actually, I can't remember whether Mrs. Kennedy had even become Mrs. Onassis as of late September 1968, let alone whether hers was the face in the newsstand that inspired me to action. It would be nice to be able to say it was. In any case, it was somebody's poor face-of-the-hour that sent me on my way in a flighty?—no, ambivalently insurgent?—yes perhaps, certainly guilt-showing, toe-tapping mood of nondirection. It was hot, I was bored, the stars of the silver screen danced temptingly across my newsreel libido—and I sensed there would be no fall session in the old folks' home for me.

"The old folks' home," how casually that slipped out, just as countless other quotes from Dylan's songs weave their way into my, our, patterns of thought. What an influence on my, our, lifestyle, what an eminently quotable source! "The old folks' home and the college," volume six, side one, band two . . . right off the top of my head. Ask me another. If there's one thing I know, it's Bob Dylan. If there's one thing I care about, it's his songs. If there's one person I'd like to . . .

"Person?"

Now, in the fall of 1968—except for a single evening's appearance at the Woody Guthrie Memorial Concert and a single LP—Bob Dylan hadn't been heard from for over two years. In July 1966, he had presumably suffered serious injuries as the result of a motorcycle accident, and no one seemed to know for sure whether he was dead or alive, maimed or an idiot. *John Wesley Harding* did appear in late '67, but was that *really* Dylan singing of saints and sinners with gunfighter ballad candor and canonical sincerity? If so, it definitely wasn't the Dylan of *Blonde on Blonde* or *Highway 61 Revisited*. Bob apparently was giving us an entire album to reaffirm one point we already knew—that he was a terrifically important figure with a huge responsibility to himself, his music, *and* his disciples. No matter what he'd previously said.

I recall the day I bought *John Wesley Harding,* I skipped an entire afternoon of good classes and listened to this strange new record until three the next morning. I devoured it the way I used to devour the Vacation and Christmastime issues of *Looney Tunes* comics; and believe me, that's fervor! I cross-checked every biblical allusion and copied my findings into a looseleaf notebook. I called friends to see what they thought. I disagreed with them, and they disagreed with me. But we loved it. There was a new testament to construe, fresh parables to ponder. There were reasons to go on.

But what was happening now? Six months or more had passed since the release of *John Wesley Harding,* and still not a word from Dylan. Secrecy enveloped him like a Carnaby Street shroud. The bait was becoming too tempting, the wait demanding beyond the furthest limits of devotion. It was time for an apocalypse.

So I initiated a program of speculation. A trip to Woodstock was unthinkable. That had been tried, never with any measurable success. Dylan wasn't about to talk to me; and besides, what would I say to him? Hey man, groove on your tunes, be my friend and I'll blow out your harmonicas . . . No, that wouldn't do. But . . . I wonder if anyone's ever been out to—where was it?—Hibbing, Minnesota, Bob's hometown. I wonder if his parents still live there. Wonder if they'd see me. Wonder. . . *if their phone number is listed with information!*

Abraham Zimmerman, Abraham Zimmerman, Abraham . . . yeah, pretty sure that's it.

"Yes, information for what city please?"

"Uh, Hibbing, Minnesota, please."

"Would you spell that please?"

"Yes, sure." I spelled it.

"Thank you. Whom are you trying to reach?"

"An Abraham Zimmerman. That's A-B-R . . ."

"Thank you. Just a moment please . . . I'm sorry, that number has been disconnected. Would you like to try another?"

"Yes, ummm . . . do you have a Zimmerman's Appliance Shop listed?" From what dark crevice of the cerebral cortex did I scrape *that* wen of Dylanformation?

"Just a moment please. . . . No, but I have a Zimmerman Furniture and Electric Company."

"That must be it!"

"The number is 2-6-3-3-6-1-5, area code 2-1-8 if you are dialing direct. Thank you."

Bob Dylan's father's business phone number! It existed; Hibbing and his father and his father's store I'd read about years ago in *Time* or *Newsweek,* they were real! I dialed the number: no answer. But of course not, it was almost midnight.

By two o'clock the next afternoon I'd screwed up the courage to try again. But what to say? I certainly had no credentials to be disturbing Abraham Zimmerman's day. Well, we'd have to make some up. Young journalist, unpublished yes, but on the way to the top . . . looking for an exclusive story, no, an exclusive *interview* with Bob Dylan's parents. Will travel. The phone was ringing.

"Hallo. Zimmerman's here."

"Hello! Hi! Is this Mr. Zimmerman?"

"This is one of 'em."

"Are you *Abraham* Zimmerman?" The connection was awful, sounded like I was talking to Alaska.

"No"—the voice softened—"Abraham Zimmerman passed away last June. This is Maurice Zimmerman."

"Oh, I see. But . . . are you Bob Dylan's *uncle?*"

"I guess I am."

What guts, Toby. If nothing else, here was a moment you could cling to as a Dylanite for the rest of your days, bum beers from for an eternity in the simple recounting of a tale. Bob Dylan's uncle, right there on the phone!

"Uh . . ."

I must have spoken with Maurice Zimmerman (pronounced "Morris") for over half an hour, and the whole time he seemed congenial, even eager to converse with someone crazy enough to call him from Washington, D.C. He was genuinely surprised at my interest in Dylan. Apparently he *wasn't* constantly besieged by reporters as I'd supposed, and, in fact, knew of only one writer who had ever even been to Hibbing. And that was a couple of years back. I kept asking Maurice Zimmerman about Dylan, but all he would say was, "Sure, he's my nephew and all, but I don't know much about him. He didn't hang around here much. Yeah, sure, I guess there are people still in town who could tell you more—kids who knew him. But not me . . . If you got questions, why don't you ask Bobby?"

Why don't I ask Bobby!

"Would you be interested in talking with me further about all this if I came out there?" I suggested meekly.

"I don't know how much I could tell you, but sure, stop by if you're in town."

"Well, thanks! How 'bout sometime next week?" T'hell with school, t'hell with a job.

"OK, fella, see you then."

TWO GUSH: *Turnpike Madness, North Country Sholom*

What I want you to do now, before we get any further, is to take out your AAA maps—starting with "North Central United States"—and see exactly how far out in the middle of everything huge and vast Hibbing, Minnesota, is. That's it, right, way up in the northeast corner of the state, the other side of Lake Superior and less than one hundred miles from the Canadian border. Wilderness, huh? Now trace that fat green line your AAA man has so efficiently stenciled down to Duluth, across the southernmost tip of Lake Superior, down through Wisconsin to northern Illinois, Chicago, and—switching to your "Northeastern United States" map—zip through the remainder of your twelve hundred mile jaunt from Hibbing, across Indiana, Ohio, Pennsylvania, Maryland, and back to Washington, D.C. Finally—now that you're home safe—imagine setting back out alone against all that concrete, for the first time, in a beat-up Volkswagen. Still with me?

Doesn't matter.

The highway *may* be for gamblers, but a wise man knows his game and never takes chances on a foolish bet. Maurice Zimmerman had allowed me one fat foot in the door of journalistic opportunity; if I played according to the rules, *anybody's* rules, I should have a story. A trip to Hibbing and a subsequent profile of the town should sell. "Site of the largest open pit iron ore mine in the world, pop. 17,731," the encyclopedias and tour books say; few people could know more about Hibbing than that. I already had the rather trollish information that Dylan's father had died the previous spring . . . did Bob come back for the funeral? Had he slipped out of reclusion to return home for services? Were the tales of Bob's total alienation from his family true, or were they prefabricated myth? Did he still have friends living in Hibbing? There had to be teachers and librarians and music store people around who would remember Bob. And what of his mother—I hadn't even thought about her! Was *she* living? In town? Hibbing couldn't help but be a gold mine.

Meanwhile, there was *the road*. A toll booth at the Breezewood entrance to the Pennsylvania Turnpike is the true beginning, of that I'm convinced. Its narrow, gun-turret chute beckons in the same irresistible posture of terror as the first length of track on the first ADULT roller-coaster ride. *Step right up, take your ticket. Try some big league driving, leave the supermarket set behind. If you can make it on this circuit, you're a pro. Step up!* . . . A true beginning to a final test . . . The Pennsylvania Turnpike twists and climbs through some of the worst industrial clatter, rock-heaviest land-scapes, and blatantly inbred culture of the East. Out-of-state radio stations tune in for five or ten miles, to be inundated quickly by static. Trucks and cars jockey for position on the viciously narrow pavement in mad attempts to get it all finished. No one wants to stop. Faces halted only by necessity at orange gasoline pumps con-tort along the lines of bad amphetamine highs. The East won't let go, won't release its hold—not without a suitably punishing gaunt-let, anyhow. The Ohio border seems centuries away.

But *finally,* there it is. The Pennsylvania VAPOS accept your cre-dentials, take your money . . . and you're free! The Ohio toll booths are just ahead, but they're tinted glass-shiny America; and behind them the entire midwestern territory stretches out in an endless wave of grain fields and Burger Chefs. Top-forty stations tune in from hundreds of miles in every direction, the turnpike widens, the sun sets, and drivers all around you settle into a groove. It's . . . America! *On the road* headed west, toying with a future in the past of some cherished mythic figure who (made to order) hitch-hiked out of the mythic Midwest to achieve mythic fame-and-fortune in a most conveniently mythic fashion. *On the road,* where strangely enough, survival depends on the tricks and rules our fathers taught us, where the State Trooper wants respect and often gets it, where the simple courtesy of blinking your lights at a passing trucker and having him blink back gives not *just* the satisfaction of knowing you understand the way the game is played, but the reassurance that if you didn't know you wouldn't make it far. (On the *side* of the road, stranded in a ditch with a handkerchief on your antenna, or wrapped pitifully around a utility pole is not what Kerouac was talking about.) *On the road,* locked into a pseudo-environment where the music of America, its news, its editorial commentary, its advertising, and its *style*—all top-forty and wham-bang—bombard you for thirteen hours a day, two to four hours at a stretch. *On the road,* where the people you pass and who pass you smile at nothing in particular, and maybe even jive in their seats to the same tune as you; where Howard Johnson's and Savarin Lounges force the traveler *back* for a few seconds into the humdrum, *back* into the negative corporeity of workadaysical *blegh. On the road,* where you can't get back out fast enough.

They tell you that if you make it all the way to Chicago the first day you've driven a stretch; but there's no inclination to stop once you've come that far. The windy-butcher city has been with you in the barker barrages of WLS and WCFL for at least three hundred miles, so when the last leg of the Indiana Turnpike slips tiredly into the Tristate Tollway and you realize that there's nothing but highway *still,* it's impossible to call it quits. The lighthouse-friendly "oases" straddling the tollway, the stopping and starting, the downshifting and upshifting out of toll booth after toll booth, and the absurd alternative of ending the day on a presanitized toilet seat in some anonymous Holiday Inn just won't let you. You need a town, a bar, a diner, some *place* you've gotten to. Chicago was your goal and you've already passed that. Strike on . . .

To Rockford, Illinois, in my case, where a clean bed in a family-run motel and a few beers at a raucously jukeboxed tavern blended comfortably into nine thirty the next morning, the Illinois border, and Wisconsin—flat and dull and paved gray past Madison to Eau

Claire, but turning quickly backwoods and twisty through the Chippewa Falls, Rice Lake, Spooner territory with nothing on the radio all day but polka music and local obituary reports. Hunting-and-fishing is a basic motif throughout northwestern Wisconsin, but the atmosphere still smacks of the East, of the East's money and big-spending vacationers. It's very...*Pennsylvanian,* very STOP HERE! EAT! Not until Duluth/Superior's WEBC starts blasting Golden Oldies down Highway 53, and Lake Superior's industrial backwash begins to delicately scent the air, do you detect a subtle difference. Your first glimpse of the lake itself cements the impression. But what? It's not James Fenimore Cooper and it's not Trenton, New Jersey. Neither is it simply another Chicago or Buffalo-on-the-bay. It's . . . the wind, the clouds, all that choppy water, freighters moored right here in the middle of America, that very corny duck winging its way north, beer ads for brands you never knew existed, a sign to Highway 61, Bob Dylan's birthplace!, steep hills, *a taste of the north country!,* something industrial, something pioneer, something European . . . something inexplicably vital.

My desire to reach Hibbing before dark was now almost sexual in its intensity. Highway 53 swept through deep pine forests chilled martini-fresh in the early fall dew, and only four towns—Twig, Canyon, Cotton, and Central Lakes—lay between me and my destination. I began watching the roadside, checking crossroads in the silly hope that I might catch, might sense the presence of our hero. Had he hitchhiked down this very stretch of road on his way to New York? Had he stood *there?* WEBC, the Golden Oldie station from Duluth, was still rocketing hits from the past, from the fifties—songs *he* drove to along this same highway, years ago, when the songs were new. I rolled down a window and filled my lungs with the fifty-degree north country air, inhaling the Valhalla-Deutsch atmosphere all Paul Bunyan and Tonio Kröger—the way a lover breathes memories from unchanged sheets.

MICROGUSH

But wouldn't you know, I almost missed the turn; there wasn't a sign. The seven o'clock sun had set a pink coral reef across Highway 37, and a tiny Harley Davidson dealer up the road lent me the only hint I was near. It was necessary to negotiate a U-turn. I stopped and asked a boy changing a tire, to make sure. I veered north on Highway 73, past huge red iron ore dumps; and that's when it happened. You won't believe me, but it did. *Dylan.* From Duluth where he was born, to Hibbing where he grew up—over that same Golden Oldie station—*Nobody feels any pain*...yes! "Just Like a Woman," harmonicas, moaning, hair as I turn west on what had to be Hibbing's main drag, the last of the sun blinding in spotlight intensity, scattering bugs on my windshield, their semi-translucent essence making it practically impossible to see, but Hibbing! Flat brown and gray buildings, dime stores, pizza parlors, street corners... *When we meet again, introduced as friends*... October air slipping up like icicles through my unsuspecting floorboards, people hustling along sidewalks bundled Christmas-tree-snug against the fall wind... *Please don't let on that you knew me when*... a shadow of the mines, huge frontier-Victorian hotel with parking lot, the ANDROY MOTOR INN, ancient Pontiacs, Fords, and Buicks bathed in red iron ore dust... *I was hungry, and it was your world*... my Volkswagen coughing to rest, collar up, glance back for an instant....

THREE GUSH: *Cardigan Nitemare, Ozzie 'n' Harriet?*

Bob Dylan's babysitter! With a real name, Don "Bud" McKenzie, right there on the next barstool! Longish gray hair, fisherman's knit T-shirt, stylishly snug black slacks tapered to ... good Christ ... elf-toed monk-strap slip-ons. In *Hibbing?* And this bar, all English Pubby and deep-cushioned Howard Johnson's in the brand-new, most *incredibly* modern Kahler Inn Towne Motel (a far cry from the Androy where I'd registered), filled with convention types, freshly coiffed midcycle women with balding guys in graveyard worsteds and shiny white shirts, all laughing, warbling "Tiny bubbles ..." around—a piano bar, an upright with one of those fake flowing Steinway bodies and the padded elbow rests, plus ... the words to all your favorite songs mimeographed for instant happy.

The bartender, a moonlighting third-grade teacher from Chisholm, was pouring Don McKenzie and me another drink. "Must be twenty years now since I last took care of Bob for Abe and Beatty," Don was saying. "He was a quiet boy, even at that age. His brother David hadn't broken in his first pair of diapers, and already you could tell that he was going to be the extrovert of the two. Bobby stayed quiet, friendly, but, well, kind of *slinky* the whole time he was growing up. Used to write poems ... don't know if he still does. But whenever Mother's Day or Father's Day or somebody's birthday rolled around, Bob would have a poem ready. Of course that was a long time before he'd ever thought of becoming Bobby Die-lan ..."

"*Die*-lan?"

"Sure, that's just the name he took so people out East wouldn't know his real name was Zimmerman. Seems a pity too, fine Jewish family name like that...and Bob was always a good Jewish boy. Went to synagogue regularly, listened to his mother and dad... but why shouldn't he, his family had more money than most. Zimmerman's Furniture and Electric used to be a good business. You have to hand it to the Jews, they're first-class moneymakers, always have been I guess, and in a small town, *they stick together*...but nobody holds that against them in Hibbing. I know I don't. And the Jews own a lot of the businesses, the movie theaters, Feldman's Department Store..."

"The movie theaters?" I tried to interject. All this was really too much. A stray conversation in the most unlikely of Hibbing settings, on the first night out, turning into this! "What about Bob's movie—was it shown here in Hibbing?"

"Didn't know he'd even made one. Funny though, you'd think if it'd played anywhere it would have played here. Especially seeing as how Bob's uncle owns the two theaters."

"*Really?* Well..."

Don McKenzie's voice dropped a few decibels, and he turned toward me with a quarter-stool swivel and a nose-bridged handcup.

"Now there's an example of how the Jews in this town take care of their own. I don't know what Bob's movie was like, but you can bet more than likely something about it wasn't exactly, well, *kosher*— or it'd been running at both theaters twenty-four hours a day, for a year."

"There *was* profanity, but..."

"You see! Now in a big town like Washington or New York or Duluth, that sort of thing wouldn't hardly scrunch 'em down in their seats. But here in Hibbing, a hometown boy like Bob, *in the movies,* with his family still living in town—except for his poor dad, bless him, as nice a fellow as you'd ever want to meet—passed away last May—and I *saw* Bobby at the wake as a matter of fact..."

"Bob was back in May?"

"Sure he was back, think he'd miss his father's funeral? He... actually the funeral itself wasn't held in Hibbing...Jews don't bury their dead in the cemetery here, they have their own over in

Duluth . . . but there was a wake right over at Dougherty's and practically everyone in town . . . Bob's close to the whole family now,
don't get me wrong. He was home for just the funeral this time
though, because his wife was expecting their third back in New
York. Named him after his father, too: Seth Abraham Isaac Dylan.
Told Beatty they decided to put the 'Isaac' in because he didn't
want the little fellow's initials to be 'S. A. D.' Yeah, Bob was home
for just a couple of days this trip. But that didn't stop him from
finding time to fix his mother up with a brand-new Cadillac and
his brother David with a Buick. Those stories you read about Bob
and his family couldn't be further from the truth. Why Beatty's
always showing off some new gift Bob's sent her—diamonds, furs—
or talking about him calling long distance from all around the
country. Like I said, Bob's a good family boy, and in Hibbing that
means something, 'cause these Jewish people, *they stick together,*
why . . ."

The din from the piano bar had gradually welled up to the point
where Don McKenzie's voice was inaudible. I tapped my ear and
shook my head, mouthing a rapid volley of WHATS? Finally Don
McKenzie's lips stopped moving, and he broke into the grandest of
smiles. Leaning closer, and with a sweeping gesture to the room,
he bellowed, "Yeah, it's a real live bunch!"

Bob Dylan's *baby*sitter?

". . . tiny bubbles. . . ."

FOUR GUSH: *Little Grace in That Gush*

Ten o'clock the next morning came with too few covers and the mercilessly insistent scream of a telephone. Where... it was... Don McKenzie, hadn't I just left him? Oh. No, he was calling from work. Apparently—at my request?—he had already been in touch with Bob's aunt this morning, asking if I might be granted an audience. The answer had been a decisive no: Unproctored interviews were not distributed by any member of the family without Bob's permission, and Beatty, Bob's mother, was in Detroit. So.

I thanked Don McKenzie, told him I'd see him later, and folded into the billows of my hangover.

The bed I'd slept in was enormous. It stretched from the door of the john, past a portable TV set, to dusty sills of three ten-foot-high windows—one of which was open six inches. I struggled with what bedclothes I possessed, and crawled down to shut it. October 2, my watch said, and the temperature had to be at least forty degrees; I was not prepared. The shower seemed icebergs away. I could see the two-foot-deep tub with its porcelain faucet levers and heavy cotton curtain, but that was in the bathroom across an imposing expanse of cold tile floor... the bathroom framed in solid oak, the oak running in polished beams along a fifteen-foot-high ceiling to the mammoth oak door, its brass latches and transom. Hibbing. The Androy Motor Inn. Me.

What had happened? Ah yes, Goodtime Evelyn, downstairs in the Androy's Crystal Lounge. Goodtime Evelyn at Hibbing's omnipresent piano bar, ooff. With me on kazoo, oh no, I hadn't really. Yes though, and with everybody singing. To Evelyn and me knocking it out; no Bobby Die-lan tunes but a whole mess of Rodgers and Hart. Evelyn had said she liked that song "Blowin' in the Wind," but I couldn't get her to play it. The place was packed. Don and I had moved from the Kahler Inn Towne to the Sportsman's Restaurant for a sandwich, and then, oh then... but what's this...

HOTEL ANDROY

"for those who like the best"

200 Rooms—2 Restaurants—Banquet Facilities—
New VIP Suites—Bamboo Room and Charcoal Corner—
Open Hearth Broiling—Supper Club—Dancing and
    Entertainment—
Hong Kong Nite Every Wednesday Evening.

—Adjacent Free Parking—

Right. An old ad on the back of an old postcard, but strikingly appropriate. The Androy was a MOTOR INN now, but still four stories high and the tallest building in town, if you could trust Don McKenzie. Everything sort of 1923 Italianate; the lobby furnished in if-you're-lucky-to-get-a-nice-one-daycoach, reflected to infinity in too many mirrors, as I recall. And I suppose the Bamboo Room is now the Crystal Lounge. With Goodtime Evelyn pounding out all your favorites.

Oh...

A strangely divergent crowd of Hibbingites had been assembled at the bar last night. The coat-and-tie set for one, older and more distinguished; the Banlon-pullover and Chino-slack set for another, arms around their girls, laughing embarrassedly; plus two or three field-jacketed, younger fellows with the look of the north woods about them, tapered to city finesse. One of the latter had approached me toward the end of the evening, introduced himself, and bought me a drink. He asked me outright what I was doing in Hibbing, so I told him. I explained how I'd talked to Maurice Zimmerman from

Washington, and how his friendliness, the lack of any previous journalistic attention having been paid to Hibbing, and my desire just to *see* what kind of a place Bob Dylan grew up in had brought me out. He was sympathetic to my interest in Dylan, if not to my plan of attack. So what, he said, if Bob came from Hibbing? So what if his mother worked over at Feldman's as a clerk? What does that have to do with his music? He thought Bob Dylan "could say it, I guess, better than *anybody*." But who cares about Hibbing? Bob could have come from anyplace.

I hadn't tried to argue with him, nor did I discourage him from sounding off about any or all. Obsessions are hard enough to explain satisfactorily to the sober; besides, I was enjoying my first encounter with the youth of Hibbing, the post-Dylan culture boom, if such existed! He was fascinating. There wasn't a shard of pretension about him. He let me have it for my intentions to perpetrate what he assumed would be a gross injustice to Dylan and his privacy, but did so in such an inoffensive manner that it in no way dulled the point of his attack, and frankly, didn't make you hate him. I felt very small, but I still liked him as much as anybody I'd met in a long while.

And it was more than just what he'd had to say, it was . . . well, the way he sat there in his field jacket at Goodtime Evelyn's piano bar, sipping his drink and expounding upon everything from the draft, to a California trip he'd recently made, to Dylan—in this clear, self-confident logic, seemingly void of hangups, that surprised me. Was this a typical Hibbingite? A young Dylan? He certainly had that classic poise . . . and concern. He was terribly worried about the draft, and feared he might have to leave the country to avoid it. He didn't want to do that . . . and he spoke of hunting, of killing deer with a bow and arrow—seven bucks, I believe he'd said—and knowing now he'd never be able to do it again. Would never want to. Killing was evil, he'd decided. We drank to that.

And drank. Don McKenzie had finally left, the Crystal Lounge was wanting to close, and he and I had said good-bye in the lobby; he with his field jacket and buddies, me with my kazoo. Headed upstairs. In the elevator I considered going out to my Volkswagen and driving home to Washington. Drunk, I'd had no desire to do evil, no wish to stick Bob in print, "starin' out at cavity minds who gobble chocolate candy bars," no mad compulsion to disturb the tranquil waters; but today. . . .

I dressed hurriedly in the warmest clothes I could find and slipped out for breakfast. Besides, it wasn't going to be like that.

HISTOROGUSH*

The Hibbing Village Chamber of Commerce is located on the first floor of the Androy, next to the barber shop—and for a dollar they'll sell you a seventy-fifth anniversary Diamond Jubilee Days illustrated souvenir booklet. They'll inform you that, yes, there have been times in Hibbing's relatively short history when the future was less than bright. The lumberjack days, for instance. Everyone thought Hibbing would die out with the timber like a hundred other Minnesota mining camps. But Frank Hibbing changed all that the day he stuck his head out of a tent on a forty-below-zero January morning in 1893 and roared, "I believe there is iron under me. My bones feel rusty and chilly."† Frank Hibbing and his miners took over the land the loggers were leaving, and "the largest red iron ore open pit mine in the world" felt the bite of its first spade.

It was rough-and-tumble from there on in—Bret Harte and Émile Zola out front, but "progress" and "culture" in the wings, as folks at the Hibbing Village Chamber of Commerce are quick to assure you. They'll give you free iron ore samples in little plastic bags, spinning mining-camp knee-slapper yarns all the while, but it won't be long before they get around to the village's more cultivated claims to national fame:

---

* From *Hibbing, Minnesota, Diamond Jubilee Days Souvenir Booklet*, p. 8.

† At this point, please cue up "North Country Blues"—*The Times They Are A-Changin'*, side one, band one. And check the album's liner notes.

Like Bob?

Bobby Die-lan? No, not exactly...

In 1919 Hibbing gave birth to the bookmobile! It was a thirty horsepower White truck, remodeled as the first library bus—to serve mining camps up and down the Mesabi Range.

The Greyhound Bus system started in Hibbing with a 1913 Hupmobile bought as a taxi by "Bus Andy" Anderson for the fifteen-cent jaunt between Alice and Hibbing. If you ask the folks at the Hibbing Village Chamber of Commerce who Hibbing's most famous citizen is, they'll tell you "Bus Andy" Anderson every time.

They'll go on to admit that, well, after World War I mining in Hibbing began to have its first serious problems. The town was still prospering. There were handsome public buildings in late Victorian Greco-Roman, fine homes for the villagers, streetcar lines, shady lanes and well-paved streets, sidewalks in front of family businesses, a healthy school system... and as Bob might say, "the lunchbucket filled every season." But prosperity threatened to devour its own, and yes, "money doesn't talk, it swears," for...

The Oliver Mining Company had obtained mineral rights to the land under the village, and was making an offer of $2,500,000 to property owners for the surface rights. Part of the deal was that eighty acres of company-owned land would be provided for development in "New" Hibbing—actually, the old mining camp Alice, one and a half miles south of "Old" Hibbing. Merchants would be allowed to choose sites in New Hibbing, three business blocks would be built by the company and sold to the merchants, and—the company would *move* one hundred and eighty-five dwellings, twelve frame business buildings, and eight *brick* business buildings... on huge iron wheels, the mile and a half from Hibbing's shady lanes and concrete sidewalks to Alice—an empty field sectioned off by a sewer pipe still above ground.

Took four years to complete the moving (*insidious* loss-of-roots-for-pure-profit-cultural schizophrenia!), and in another six years the Depression had hit and New-Old Hibbing faced a different kind of potential annihilation: Mining came to a near standstill.

But the village survived. And World War II came along. That didn't help matters much, but at least the mines were working again. Though day by day they were becoming too expensive to operate, ore was no longer plentiful, the few men left in the mines before the war were being drafted . . . women took over in the pits—shades of *Germinal*—and the profit was next to nil. After the war, well how you gonna keep 'em down in the mines, but . . . TACONITE changed all that.

A low-grade iron ore, approximately 27 percent iron and 51 percent silica, that United States Steel began investigating five or six years previous as a possible solution to the critical ore shortage on the Mesabi Range. The result: Geologists say there is a sufficient quantity of taconite available along the range to last for more than one hundred years. Taconite, it seems, was virtually worthless as a raw material for the steel industry until recently when research . . . But the times have changed, both mines and plants operate regularly, Hibbing's prosperity once again blossoms with Kahler Inn Towne motels and junior colleges, two snowmobiles in every garage,

A GLORIOUS PAST

A BRILLIANT PRESENT

AN EXCITING FUTURE!

FIVE GUSH: *Bums a Dime, in Your Prime*

Two inverted red iron canyons gouging pink tears in the sky at either main street extremity. Huge rusty mounds sloping off to miles of moon-crater cavities, in three out of four directions. East, west, and... north to abandoned Old Hibbing. There are four houses left in the old town, I'm told; all public buildings have been demolished. But their absence couldn't be the most oppressive factor. It's the land, the pit.

And the sky itself. Heavy cloud formations hanging over the village, to the roofs of buildings. Big gray monsters that look a ton apiece—even when the sun is brightest. A cold sky. With real rainbows and north country sunsets, but freezing cold. Even then, in early fall, when the temperature still hit the sixties.

A mountaintop atmosphere, with a dash of the sea in a wind that never stops blowing; and snow so many months. Snowmobiles! They seemed more popular than cars as I strolled on up Howard Street (the village's main drag) from the Androy, past the Jolly Rodger and Sportsmen's cafés to Ace Hardware, Woolworth's, and Montgomery Ward's. Snowmobiles were on display there, sleek, and up to *fifty* horsepower... as much as a Volkswagen. You have your Ski-Doos, your Panther Arctic Cats—and over at the First National Bank, a Johnson Skee-Horse right in the window! Special offer. Big contest.

And the physical layout of the town. All the shops and public buildings on Howard Street are low profile. It's a strange effect. Take

Feldman's, for instance, where Bob's mother worked. It's the biggest department store in town, yet only two stories high and flat-roofed, like a dime store. One scans the horizon uncomfortably for a skyscraper... and catches the four stories of the Androy.

Where to begin? Where to start mining particles of a man's past, all the basketball shoes and cheeseburgers and TV Saturday mornings which cement the whole? There are the obvious people and places: his school, his library, his newspaper, his music store and music teachers?, his hangouts, his mechanics? his house! My god, his friends, his relatives, his enemies? his father's business, yes, my friend, his uncle!

A right off Howard Street down Fifth Avenue, the Androy's desk clerk has informed me, across the street and... ah-ha, Zimmerman's Furniture and Electric!, the family business, just another two-story affair, pink on the bottom, brown and the "Kay Hotel" on top, rooms-to-let more like it I supposed, tired, dirty miners on a Friday night binge... but downstairs, all furniture and appliances — refrigerators and stoves, sofas and dining room suites, plus Maurice Zimmerman waving quizzically from the counter of a small electronics repair shop.

Maurice shook my hand, introduced his brother Paul, and all three of us stood there for a few seconds looking embarrassed. Maurice and Paul ran the store now; Abe had been a partner; Maurice is the oldest brother, starting to gray, and cigar-mouthed rotund; Paul is still very dark, and less friendly than Maurice; although Maurice was hesitant — like Bob's aunt, Mrs. Edelstein — to speak of Bob:

"He's my nephew, sure, like I told you... but I don't know much about him. He never hung around here much. Left town pretty young. I saw him some when he was a boy, but not much. He used to sweep the shop sometimes. For change, fifteen cents or a quarter, but he never really worked at the store like they said in the magazines. His father worked here, with Paul and me. But that's all. Bobby was quiet. And independent — like when he quit school. Came home from Minneapolis and told his parents he wanted to go to New York, to try and make it on his own. Didn't want any help, just took enough money from his father to get East, no more. His mother, she could tell you most about that. But she's not in town now, she's traveling. I can't tell you much. He just didn't hang around here. No, I never knew much about him. None of us did."

That's it?

"Well, some of us got pretty upset when he said certain things about the town. Almost like he was ashamed. He had no call to do that, to say he didn't know his family... and that the town was dying." He turned to me. "How 'bout it fella, tell 'em the truth. Tell 'em Hibbing's not dead."

OK, Mr. Zimmerman, and thanks as I hustled back out onto Fifth Avenue, out of the dusty past for a while and up toward Howard Street, in search of... a *little* of Hibbing's new-found, never-lost? prosperity for Bob. Past Woolworth's, Montgomery Ward's, and Sears, where nary a Famous Face or Personality Poster applauded the worldwide notoriety of our hometown hero. Where *Bob Dylan's Greatest Hits* was the only album of Bob's in stock, and where smiling salesladies offered me sticky-stringed renditions of "Blowin' in the Wind" by the Muzak Strains of Jehovah Seventeen or somesuch. But... of course, to Crippa's! Howard Street's only full-fledged music store, and surefire dealer for... *two* of Bob's records? *John Wesley Harding* and the *Greatest Hits*. None of the fine old stuff on early albums about Hibbing and the north country? Neither of the folk-rock albums, *Bringin' It All Back Home* and *Highway 61 Revisited,* the two that *crucified* popular music....

The saleslady at Crippa's explained that, well, Bob doesn't sell too well in Hibbing. People don't like his voice. Some of the other groups that do his songs—The Byrds; Peter, Paul, and Mary; Joan Baez—they sell a whole lot better. But Saleslady likes Bob. She sold him his first harmonica. And harmonica rack! Had to order that special, she didn't have the faintest idea... Bob had had to draw her a picture. Sure, he was in Crippa's quite often; from the time he was just a little boy. Always fascinated by music. Would spend hours in the store listening to records . . . all kinds. He liked classical music at first, but sometime during his junior high school years he got interested in popular music. Blues, country, rock and roll . . . everything.

A dark-haired fellow with a quick stride and intense gaze emerged from a back office, and Saleslady introduced me in an off-hand fashion to Chet Crippa, the store's proprietor. Chet was friendly and eager to talk about Bob, interested in what he was doing, and slightly embarrassed that only two of Bob's albums were selling in Hibbing. Chet reiterated much of what Saleslady had already told me, adding enthusiastically that yes, he could remember Bob's interest in country music at an early age, having had to order all of Hank Williams's records for him at one fell swoop. Chet had outfitted Bob's rock band, too.

Bob's *rock band?*

Sure, he and some of the other kids had a band. Chet had supplied them all with the necessary stuff—amplifiers, mikes, guitars . . . right down to picks and strings. In those days apparently, Bob carried his guitar with him wherever he went. An old beat-up Sears and Roebuck job, with a leather strap. Slung it over his shoulder and down his back . . . through snowstorms and everything. Yes, Bob had been in Crippa's a lot. Nice kid. Talented.

On up Howard Street, toward the Hibbing *Daily Tribune* and *certainly* a complete file on our hero, perhaps even a ticker tape hotline to Grossman's office in New York, who knows?—but first, I checked for signs of the wicked messenger at every crossroad. And café. Into Mr. Jack's, the L & B, Edwardsons', and Sammy's Pizza Palace. Straight to the jukebox. But . . . not a Wurlitzer in town with a Dylan tune. Not one! Beatles, Bee Gees, and Bobby Goldsboro—but no Bobby Die-lan. And these were places where the kids hung out. The kids! Sammy's Pizza Palace, for instance. A classic malt shop. No beer with your pizza there, just soda pop and coffee. No tables either, but wooden booths—like in an *Archie* comic book. Stuffed deer heads and poorly mounted walleyed pike for decor. But good coffee. The kids drink a lot of it, four or five cups for their fifteen cents. The kids were friendly and looked like kids most places except . . . for their dress. The girls were fairly up-to-date, department-store tweed. No boutique fashions or hippy garb, to be sure. But rather stylish, nonetheless. The boys were the very opposite. Big pompadours with gobs of Brylcream, gabardine sport shirts tucked into black slacks cinched up by skinny silver belts, white socks, and black loafers with . . . horseshoe taps! Join the Elvis rebellion. Circa 1956.

There didn't appear to be any hippies in Hibbing. God forbid. The kids told a story that last time Bob was in town, not for his father's funeral, but before that, he came into Sammy's for a pizza. Hardly anyone recognized him at first. He just walked over by the counter to wait in line for his pizza. But then some girl sort of screamed, and everybody started giggling and making remarks. Bob got out of there pretty fast. But the funny thing was, not the fact that there was Bobby Die-lan right here in Sammy's Pizza Palace, but the way . . . he looked. That *hair*, and those . . . *clothes*. Nobody had ever, I mean it was spooky the way everyone spaced out over this weird little man. Who just happened to be Bobby Die-lan.

The kids at Sammy's didn't have much more to say about Bob. They'd rather talk about four-barrel carburetors or fuel injection. The hot-rod thing, another late 1950s early 1960s vogue. Popular music seems harder to come by in Minnesota than most places. The local station plays no rock, just polkas and Andy Williams Muzak (I had met Keith Knox, WMFG's program director, at Crippa's, and he had assured me that the station did have a copy of *John Wesley Harding* and a Mantovani record with Bob's music on it, somewhere), and the only top-forty station you can pick up during daylight hours is WEBC from Duluth. And that's not really top forty, but Golden Oldie. The big midwestern stations with solid top-forty formats all tune in at night—but fairly late and somehow sounding very far away.

Consequently, one wondered. About Bob, in the middle fifties, when rock music was still struggling for play on big stations back East. And what it must have been like musically in Minnesota *then*.

The Hibbing *Daily Tribune* didn't have the answer. First thing they asked was "What's Bobby doing now?" All they had on file was one picture...a four- or five-year-old publicity shot...and no real write-ups. The society-page editor didn't disappoint me though, she came through with a tacky rumor or two concerning Bob's return for the funeral. She told me David, Bob's brother, had been married about a month ago and that the family hadn't even announced it. David was married over in the Blessed Sacrament Church, you see. Oh yes, I saw. Did she or Mr. Ackerson there at his desk, pipe in hand, shifting, listening, looking dangerously intelligent, have anything else pertinent on file? Yes, one of Mr. Ackerson's columns about David and *his* music—gleaned from a story in the Minneapolis *Tribune*. An attractive assistant something, Lynn Fena, smiled, looked impressed with the import of my mission, and retrieved a copy...plus Abraham Zimmerman's obituary. Exactly! Very strange. Just a small bio, no mention of Bob except that Mr. Zimmerman's

> survivors are his wife, Beatrice; two sons Bob Dylan, Woodstock, N.Y.; David, Minneapolis; four brothers, Maurice and Paul, both of Hibbing; Jack, Virginia, and Max, Van Nuys, Calif.; a sister, Mrs. Louis (Marion) Kenner, Duluth, and three grandchildren.

The fact that Abraham Zimmerman had been a partner in the firm of Zimmerman Furniture and Electric Company and a member of Agudath Achim Synagogue, B'nai B'rith, the M.A.A., and the Hibbing Rotary Club was obviously more important to the citizens of Hibbing than any mention of Bob's laurels. But...Bob, according to the society-page editor, had never bothered to forward any press releases to his hometown paper. They had tried to keep up at first, but after Bob made his first derogatory statements about Hibbing for the national news mags, well....

Mrs. Janey Dixon over at the public library was very nice, too, even apologizing for not having any of Bob's records or songbooks on the shelves. Not even a file of clippings. But there sat the Daniel Kramer picture book! Mrs. Dixon knew Bob's parents and family, of course, but didn't have any real information on Bob. She remembered him; he had been around. But this was a new library. No, there was no way to try and trace what books Bob might have been checking out. They were under a different system now. Mrs. Dixon made a few phone calls for me; but everyone she could think of who might have known Bob was out of town. Or had moved away.

SIX GUSH: *Got the C—, Angel Baby, Nitty-Gritty, Blues*

It's tough to stay outside for very long in Hibbing, especially once the sun has started to go down. It's impossible to negotiate Howard Street. The sun sets like a pencil-beam headlight at the west end of town, giving off little enough heat but the most intense inland light I've ever encountered. What it must be like with snow as an added reflector. But darkness comes fast in October, chilling the ever-present wind and driving one repeatedly inside for coffee after coffee until the inevitable . . . give up, ride it on out in the Crystal Lounge, the Kahler's Pub room, the Jolly Rodger, *anyplace* you can get a drink and brood over your north country cold and the merciless weather.

Four or five old men were clustered around a similarly aged television set in the Androy's lobby as I came off the street; they were watching the World Series. Sports are big in Hibbing, especially baseball. Roger Maris is from Hibbing. Somebody asked me why I was wasting my time on Bobby Die-lan when I could be writing about Roger. Well, I don't know. It's not that I disapprove of sports writing, it's just that I never could stand Roger Maris. Zero class. What a bum to have taken the title from the Babe. Maris always wore his Yankee pinstripes like a pair of dirty coveralls, and that black glove on his left hand makes him look even more the laborer—like the hard-ass who wears leather wrist supports while he's jockeying a wheelbarrow or digging a trench. Gary Puckett is from Hibbing, too. And Gino Pelucci, the fellow who started Chun

King foods and who almost bought the Washington Senators last year. A brilliant past, an exciting...

Waiting at the bar of the Crystal Lounge for B. J. Rolfzen, Bob's eleventh-grade English teacher, trying to forget about outside and then for a while, luxuriating in a tall glass of Grain Belt Premium beer, "Been a Long Time a-Brewing,'" that's what it says, right there on the label. Absolutely the best American beer I've ever had; you can't get it back East. Bert Ackerson and Society-page Editor over at the *Tribune* told me that B. J. would be my best bet from the high school. He had seemed eager to talk when I called him. Said he felt it was almost his duty to see people like me who were interested in Bob. Apparently I wasn't the first after all. B. J. had mentioned somebody from the New York *Times*—probably Robert Shelton. I'd been looking for his book since 1966, but it had never appeared. It was supposed to. Was I going to be scooped, when his book came out in the midst of my endeavors, would it all be rendered worthless? Maybe in terms of my career, but certainly not in terms of my psyche. A bar in Hibbing, Minnesota! Bob Dylan's eleventh-grade English teacher!

Lena Ricci, the Androy's night clerk who had been so nice to me when I checked in (everybody's nice), and who had showed me how to get to Zimmerman's, also told me she could remember Bob's father bringing in Bobby and David to the Androy's restaurant for Sunday dinner—the boys dressed up and looking handsome. Abe had been the nicest, most friendly man in town, Lena said. He had been so proud of Bob...always coming in for the magazines, to check and see if Bob was being mentioned. All that publicity about Bob and drugs had hurt Abe. People were talking, and it was hard. But...Lena would never forget the three of them, Abe, Bobby, and David coming in for Sunday dinner.

Well, there I was. Neither dressed up nor particularly handsome, but in the same spot, waiting for Bob's teacher (sure hope he drinks, doesn't mind *me* drinking), and starting to feel... trapped? Hibbing?

But, B. J. Rolfzen. In a tan raincoat and conservative suit, a youngish fellow, lean, with dark hair. Outgoingly friendly and bemused.

At scruffy me? Or the possibilities of immortality for Bobby Zimmerman? No, not Bobby, Robert. The boy next door. Almost literally. B. J. had lived across the street from Bob during the high school years. Excuse me—Robert. Robert was a quiet boy, aloof. Used to sit in the front row of B. J.'s class, to the left of the desk. Never said a word, just listened. Got good grades, B plusses. . . . Took life seriously. Spent a lot of time by himself, must have been thinking and writing—though B. J. never saw anything young Robert produced. Liked motorcycles, had a slew of them. And to have owned a motorcycle in the middle fifties, one would've *had* to be considered . . . well, could never have labeled Robert wild or *hoody* . . . he was always such a sharp dresser . . . but perhaps, *eccentric.* The rock band he and some of the other kids had, for instance. Yes, that was quite a band. Electric. Folk music was far from fashionable in those days. Rock and roll was king, and even that was new to Hibbing. One of the biggest shocks of B. J.'s life was the first time Robert and the band performed at a school concert. Eleventh grade, the Jacket Jamboree Talent Festival. Curtain went up, Robert gave the signal, and *absolutely* the loudest music anybody had ever heard . . . and Robert! *Standing up* at the piano, screaming this . . . music into three microphones, this quietest of boys from the front row of B. J.'s English class, bellowing like . . . a *Negro* or something, with the rest of the band, two electric guitars, a bass and drums just splitting your ears, and. . . . Why, the principal told B. J. later that Robert had pounded so hard on the Baldwin's fortissimo pedal that he'd broken it off.

Positively Dionysian. That silent boy. And the way he acted the next day! Sat in his usual seat in the front row of B. J.'s English class, didn't say anything, but . . . smirked the entire period. As if to say, that's right, B. J. You saw it. And you can be a witness.

(B. J. Rolfzen didn't drink—at least not in my company. I signaled the bartender frantically for another Grain Belt. B. J. wouldn't even take a cup of coffee. He just smiled grimly at my interruption, nodded politely at my rescued "Cheers," and continued.)

Vachel Lindsay's the American poet B. J. considers closest to Robert. In style. And tradition.

> William Sanzinger killed poor Hattie Carroll
> with a boomlay, boomlay, boomlay Boom. . . .

Maybe. And "the ladder of law has no top and no bottom," B. J. said he liked that line. Plus the dust-jacket poetry of *The Times They Are A-Changin'*, the part about Hibbing, B. J. assigns that to his eleventh-grade class every year. Those lines about the courthouse and the church with its arms cut off in the moonlight . . . beautiful stuff. And "With God on Our Side," unquestionably Robert's finest song. B. J. never fails to play that one for the class, discusses it, tries to show exactly how . . . and they always ask so many questions. What *was* this Bobby Die-lan like? Did he really sit right *there?*

Sure, B. J. saw Robert when he was back last visit—for his father's funeral. But not at the funeral parlor. Over at the Zimmermans'. All the Zimmermans were there, Maurice and Paul, their families, the Edelsteins, the Goldfines . . . B. J. spoke to each of them, lingering with Beatty and David. But where's Robert? Didn't he? . . . Oh yes, David explains, of course he's home. Back in the kitchen, you know . . . by himself.

Not a bit surprised, B. J. assures me. Robert always was a loner. Even around the house. B. J. excuses himself from those assembled in the living room, and walks back to the kitchen. All the way through, way off to the left in the breakfast nook . . . there's Robert. Just sitting. Smoking a cigarette. Recognizes B. J. at once, though. Stands to greet him with a firm handshake. B. J.'s impressed. Robert always did have such fine manners. And you know how many kids *today* would . . . but Robert's embarrassed, and yes, thank you, you're very kind, but . . . quickly shifts the conversation to B. J. and Hibbing. How's the class? Things still the same over at school? Miss it in a way . . . have you heard my latest album, *John Wesley Harding?* No, B. J. replies, hasn't gotten around to it yet. But will first chance. Robert still shaking B. J.'s hand and standing calm, blue-eyed in the middle of the kitchen—goes on to say, well yes, uh, wish you would. Think it's my best . . . and after all, Mr. Rolfzen, I do believe you owe me as much. What's that?, slight

flush... 'Cause *you,* Mr. Rolfzen—a hint of the old smirk from front row, left center—*you're the one taught me everything I know.*
... Great *christ,* Bob!...

Yes, B. J. Rolfzen. Sitting modestly across the table from me in the Androy's Crystal Lounge. He was finally silent, lost in reverie... and in peace. There was nothing left to say. I signaled the waitress for our check. *My* check. While Goodtime Evelyn over at the piano bar swung into something sentimental.

SEVEN GUSH: *And a Thousand Miles Behind*

I still hadn't seen Bob's house. I knew where it was, over on East Seventh Avenue at the corner of Twenty-fifth Street. Don McKenzie had told me that. I couldn't, wasn't ready to go there yet. It had rained in the night and a light fog hung in Howard Street; breakfast at the Sportsmen was extra hot. Villagers crowded into booths all around me, huddling out of the chill, smiling, laughing too much. The waitress gave me a free cup of coffee with my eggs and I had to ask twice for a check. Nobody was in a hurry to go back outside today. I had to see North Hibbing.

East Third Avenue runs north out of Hibbing two blocks to a single-lane wooden bridge that crosses tracks of the Great Northern Railroad at Industrial Street, and separates the old from the new. A potholed, muddy trail takes over there, winding past mining-company-official buildings, a mammoth iron ore dump, and the old village cemetery—still green and peaceful, but a frightened anachronism with Rust mine at its maw. The mines are everywhere now, Agnew, Hull...and on all three sides of East Third Avenue. The old road and what few yards of land that still surround it stretch out into the abyss like a Nantucket jetty. But without the jetty's comforting sensation of permanence. A company truck might rumble past, but by October the mines have closed for the winter. The man may look menacing at first, but your out-of-state tags will assure him you mean no harm, probably aren't a vandal. He should let you continue—on up to the Hull-Rust viewing site, over and around the foot-deep potholes, the red gravel, and the mud—to what's left of the old town. A square chunk of land, maybe two acres, bordered on every side by some reminder of the mines' gnawing presence: the railroad directly to the north, a huge company shack to the west, ore dumps to the east and south, and beyond... endless excavation, tunnels, pits, unnatural lakes, and stalled machinery; draglines, shovels, and gigantic tractors. All bathed in a fine red dust.

The morning I stood next to the big Hull-Rust observation tower and looked out at the pit, the fog was too heavy for me to tell exactly how far it extended. I could see maybe two or three miles in each direction, and there was no end in sight at that distance. Just an infinity of tall, fat dumps and the land chopped up like a bad complexion. Not a person for miles, nor a sound....

Only three houses stood in the old town, not four as I'd been told. The three sisters squatted together at the southwest end of Old Hibbing, as far from the excavations as possible. Their frame walls, once white or pale blue with a fresh coat of paint, had long since succumbed to the rusty red of a heavily ored wind. Cement walks to nowhere crept out from their porches. Foundations yawned. North Hibbing's cemetery was all that stayed green; the earth had been cheated. I hurried back to my Volkswagen and fired up the heater... a child at the seashore, poking the flesh of a dead fish.

Back at the Androy, curled comfortably around a hot buttered rum in the Crystal Lounge, I came across the following tale. It was tucked way back on page fifty-four of the *Hibbing, Minnesota, Diamond Jubilee Days Souvenir Booklet,* under the heading KICKING MULE CREATES CONTROL. From the St. Paul *Dispatch,* May 20, 1918:

> For Fate had written that things were to change. Down near the edge of Sellers' open-pit mine lived a Swede named Iver Lind. Lind owned a span of Kentucky mules. These animals, lean and angular,

powerful and stubborn, were Lind's choicest possession. Long ago they had become accustomed to the din of the dynamite and the steam shovel.

One morning Lind was harnessing his mules, preparatory to starting his day's labors. Half harnessed they were, and Lind was sweating and swearing over their stubbornness, congratulating himself, withal, upon owning such a perfect span when suddenly the whistle in the Sellers' mine blew a warning note.

A blast was due. It was too late for either Iver or his mules to get to shelter.

Bang. The blast tore loose. It sent a barrage of stones and gravel high in the air. One of the descending rocks struck one of Lind's mules.

This was something to which the mule had never become accustomed. With a kick and a bray he broke loose. The bray filled the air, while the kick found lodgment in Lind's anatomy.

Iver was full of wrath. First, the mules and then the mining company was to feel the weight of his anger. Into the barn, with accompanying blows and curses, went the mules. To the office of power went Iver.

At once the Swede wanted to start injunction proceedings against the Sellers' Mining Company. The ensuing action affected only Lind's property, but its results were far-reaching.

It started a legal battle in Hibbing which extended over several years, and attracted and aroused the interest of the entire country.

Here are some of the results of the suit, and the resultant injunction:

    a. It cost the mining companies several million dollars, they now admit.

    b. It paved every street in Hibbing.

    c. Likewise, in every street it installed a white-way.

    d. It woke the people of Hibbing up with a start.

    e. It brought them a clearer realization of a number of problems affecting their welfare than they ever had before.

    f. It roused the Hibbing spirit, and that sustained the people of Hibbing through one of the most trying periods in the history of the town.

    g. It put thousands of dollars into the pockets of the people, who are disposing of their holdings on the "north forty."

It is the best thing all round, that ever happened to Hibbing, and everybody realizes it now.

And so, with an injunction growing out of a kick of a mule, peace, comparative quiet, and much prosperity came to Hibbing.

I tossed back another hot drink and ordered lunch: a fat, toasty-brown walleyed pike, with a piece of parsley in its ear.

EIGHT GUSH: *Hang Around an Ink Well*

It was about one thirty when I drove up in front of Hibbing High School, and kids were lounging against the flagpole and draped across the several tiers of concrete steps that led up to the main entrance. I parked my car across from a little snack shop on Seventh Avenue and tried to ease casually down an off sidewalk to the huge front door. But I was spotted. First titters, then clearly audible, smart-aleck remarks—in my leather jacket and heavy wool turtleneck, I guess I didn't look much like a Hibbingite. They were all in shirtsleeves and blouses! And my hair, too. Not long by normal standards, but today, *well,* windblown and a mite freaky. Some of the kids I recognized from Sammy's Pizza Palace, and we smiled. But I didn't want to linger. I mean, good lord, Bob Dylan's high school was right there waiting.

I had the names of two or three teachers I could use for reference, that is, if anybody was going to give me a hard time, but what the heck, I just wanted to explore. The school was a monster. It spread out for blocks; and inside, the marble and brass and polished wood went on and on. A mean-looking older guy, with the air of an official monitor, was shushing kids in the main hall as I came in, but he didn't have the nerve to question. I had my camera slung over my shoulder, and appeared very professional. Besides, those people never keep out real troublemakers.

A study hall was in session at the far end of the main corridor. I stood to one side and watched the kids at their desks—ancient wooden ones, a parody of themselves. The kids fidgeted and kicked and silently snickered at their proctor just like kids did when I was in school. And Bob, I'm sure. Some of them were studying, but the majority were preoccupied with more important things . . . the girl in the next row, that fat kid with the pimples on his neck up front, a gray sky pasted in the window. Would it snow? The restrooms were still as popular as I remembered them being in my day, and a steady flow of starched chinos, monogrammed sweaters, and looseleaf notebooks whisked by me in restless satisfaction. Things couldn't have changed much.

I wandered down the main hall and took a right at the end toward some administratively plaqued doors . . . the principal's office? Why not, I had names to toss around. And after all, I was a bonafide freelance writer, covering the coast-to-coast Bobby Die-lan story. But . . .

Bob Dylan's high school yearbook! With Bob Dylan's principal Ken Pederson standing over me in Bob Dylan's principal's office, a youngish fellow and nice like B. J. Rolfzen and everybody else . . . but

> *Robert Zimmerman:*
>
> "To join Little Richard"—
> Latin Club 2;
> Social Studies Club 4.

To join *Little Richard?* Oh blasphemous myopia of yearbook volunteers the world over . . . and Bob Dylan, a member of the Social Studies Club? The Latin Club, *maybe,* but the Social Studies Club . . . a bunch of Friday afternoon kids sitting around discussing this week's *Senior Scholastic?*

And . . . no, I couldn't believe it . . . Bob Dylan's report card! Principal was being careful not to let me see any grades, but I asked to take a closer look at that incredible junior high school picture pasted to the transcript—some fat little kid with greasy hair and a plaid flannel sport shirt, *beyond* further description—and quickly glanced down the list of grades. Ones I saw: average as apple pie, with some Bs in English. English had been consistently Bob's best subject, Principal informed me. I immediately asked about Bob's attendance record, and Principal assured me it had been excellent. What about all those times Bob was supposed to have run away, then? Had he been extra careful to pick vacations?

"Well," Principal said, "for a while there, when Bob was just getting started in show business . . . you know, building an image . . . the family asked us not to divulge any information that might . . . *contradict* his press releases. But now, Bob no longer seems to fear admission of his rather normal childhood in Hibbing, and the family has given us the OK to come out and speak freely."

Hmmm. Had the high school kept a file on their 1959 graduate? As a matter of fact, yes. Apparently Hibbing High School had been chosen this year for the Francis Bellamy Award, a national prize for the state (Minnesota in 1968) high school whose spirit most genuinely reflected that of Francis Bellamy—the author of the Pledge of Allegiance to the Flag. A key consideration of the Bellamy Award Committee is the list of noteworthy alumni submitted by an eligible high school . . . the notables' stature as American citizens, the patriotic cast of their lifestyles, etc. Bob's name appeared on the Hibbing High School roster, tucked way back among his fellow alumni's laurels:

NAME	ACHIEVEMENT	GRADUATION DATE
Bob Dylan	Modern folk song writer and singer. His fame and fortune was made with the singing of his ballad "Blowin' in the Wind" by Peter, Paul, and Mary. A millionaire at 25 years of age. Reached the top within six months after his arrival in New York.	June 5, 1959

I couldn't keep from wondering, cynic that I am, what might have happened in the finals if Hibbing High had included Bob's big political statement in the March 1966 *Playboy* "Interview": Asked hypothetically what legislation he might encourage if elected president of the United States, Bob promised to "immediately re-write *The Star Spangled Banner,* and little schoolchildren, instead of memorizing *America the Beautiful,* would have to memorize 'Desolation Row.'" Shocking facetiousness! And enough to make old Francis Bellamy roll right over in his flag.

But the prize had been won, danger of debauchery had passed, and kids up and down the halls were polishing trophies and plaques for the acceptance ceremonies, as Principal ushered me downstairs to meet Val Peterson, Bob's junior high school music teacher. Bob had returned to his alma mater, by the way . . . for David's gradua-tion. Principal didn't remember precisely when that was, but sev-eral years back when Bob was at the height of his popularity. Had songs on the radio and all that. Very few people to this day know Bob was in the audience. His hair was long then, and he was eas-ily recognizable . . . they had waited until the ceremonies began and slipped him into a back row. He'd snuck out just before the end, and hardly anybody even saw him; but he'd been there, for his brother's graduation.

We caught Val Peterson, an attractive, jovial woman alive with rhythm and musical smiles, at her desk in the classroom that had been hers since Bob was a music student at HJH. She greeted me laughing—oh yes, Bobby, he sat right over there. In the front row. (I sat down. The desk was tiny and cramped, with a light tan top worn smooth by the elbows of who-knows-how-many generations. I wrapped the back of my knee over a metal strut, took out my notebook, leaned forward, and grooved on the marble coolness of Bobby Zimmerman's seat.) Bob had been an able student, always participated well in class . . . though he was never exceptional gradewise. Would do his course work but never really got a good grade in something unless that something excited him. Once you got him excited, well, it was tough to rein him in. His brother David, on the other hand . . . just the opposite. An excellent student, steady worker, and fine pianist. But classical, strictly. Now *that* boy could make his living from the piano.

Bob had been interested in classical music, too. Though earlier in his student career. Pop music became big for him . . . oh, the first year of high school. He played guitar and piano then, and whenever the school had a music show scheduled, Bob would be there, whether he was invited or not. His audiences didn't take him very seriously in those days, Val Peterson fears. They didn't understand what he was trying to do . . . re-create the harshness of the country, folk, and blues idioms. Bob performed by himself primarily. Without the band. He always had marvelous stage presence, was a natural. But people didn't care. His sound was grating, and they didn't like it. Bob finally did achieve a certain degree of notoriety in Hibbing, however: He came in third one year at the Winter Frolic Talent Competition.

Of course Val Peterson is fond of Bob's music! She plays his records for the class and proudly answers the same questions that besiege B. J. Rolfzen. She seems more aware of Bob's influence on popular music, though. Uses terms like folk-rock, mentions key groups by name . . . and her version of the infamous first school appearance of Electric Bob is by far the best.

But to the scene of the crime. The Hibbing High School Auditorium, 1957. The Jacket Jamboree Talent Festival and Bobby Zimmerman. Hibbing's original blue-eyed soul brother, on dirty-blues piano, *standing up* for our pleasure, the heir to Fats Domino, Chuck Berry, Buddy Holly, *Little Richard.* . . .

The auditorium—theater in truth, modeled after the Capitol Theater in New York, scaled down to village size, Principal tells me—cost millions to build, with the plushest seats, most expensive drapes, finest musical instruments, the best in sound equipment . . . sound equipment! According to Val Peterson: Electric Bob, mad for volume, decides that the group's several microphones and amplifiers just won't do the job. It's a big hall and Bob wants to blow these Philistines out of their Capitol Theater seats. Make it loud enough to mess up a few accordion-player, seven-man-pyramid, talent-show minds. Fast and hard enough to get right in there and destroy some brain cells.

So when the curtain rises, there's Bob and the group, with not only their own sound equipment up full, but the *entire* school amplification system as well. Mikes in the piano, on amplifiers, in front of the bass drum...and *three* at Bob's side for the vocal. *KA-WHANG-ang-ang!* There is...confusion somehow, people are...disoriented and...no one's able to react in a fashion...appropriate.... Principal in the first row, host to school-system officials and visiting Iron Range dignitaries...*fights*...his way backstage and...halfway through Bob's first number cuts the house mikes with the flick of a switch. It's still *plenty* loud out there, but Bob's hopping mad. (Maybe that's when he broke the foot pedal on the Baldwin. Some piano. Still right onstage, sheathed in a gray quilted cover.) Anyway, Bob finishes his set and stalks offstage; amid shocked and indignant laughter, at music these villagers have never heard the *likes* of...and Bob's voice. A garbled howl—they chuckle. Sure wasn't *singing*, guffaw. Bob didn't speak to anyone at school for days.

NINE GUSH: *No Direction Home*

So long to Hibbing High, the Bellamy Award, and Principal. Through hallowed Doric columns into an early October snow flurry. A northwest wind blowing hard and wet as I trudged down Seventh Avenue . . . a street Bob must have walked thousands of times on his way to and from school. I hesitated for a moment at the school's fence, staring out at the empty football field, the bleachers, and the asphalt track. "The only trouble with playin' guitar is that you can't get the cheerleader girls," Bob had once told a *Time* reporter, and that seemed the saddest of understatements here at the high school's back door . . . in the slush, puddles of black cinders where the fall chalk had melted. It must have been hard passing that field every morning on the way to B. J. Rolfzen's English class; and harder coming back, the afternoon firm and shiny with the grace of uncensored, uncut athletic performances . . . their cheering audiences an aesthetic mockery to Bobby's efforts to entertain. Maybe not, though. Maybe he just shut his eyes and ears and didn't bother to care. I let go of the Cyclone fence and headed on down the street, past the Blessed Sacrament Church where David had been married last summer, to . . . 2425 East Seventh Avenue, at the corner of Twenty-fifth Street . . . the Zimmerman family residence and . . . the house where Bob grew up!

A strange-looking house. Rectangular in shape, under a flat roof—like a garage-attached Greek temple, with pseudo-classical moldings and a column-lacking portico. All done in light tan stucco, behind a yard full of fat bushes. Neighboring houses are somehow less impressive. They run the gamut: from B. J. Rolfzen's ex-residence across the street, a little pink cottage rambling off in all directions ... to big split-level types around and about—to the house right next door, more than a bit ramshackle. Plus Twenty-fifth Street torn up by construction and partially closed to traffic—all lend the Zimmermans' place an air of permanence.

I stood across Seventh Avenue, taking it in. Street signs, sidewalks, trees, a mailbox—things around a neighborhood that matter only to the people who have lived with them. They are things that don't change much. Things one can almost count on still being there, when and if one decides to return.

Thoughts strayed back to North Hibbing where no such mementos survived ... but not for long. Maybe Bob's mother was back. Or had never left. The wind was howling, snow blasting about, "darkness at the break of noon," and there's a pilgrim at your door Miz' Zimmerman, needs shelter from this storm.

Mrs. Zimmerman? Angel Marolt, a young housewife with a couple of kids peeking out from behind her legs. I should have known better; the screen door was hanging open and a black Thunderbird perched in the drive. I asked about Mrs. Zimmerman. Nope, she didn't live here anymore. *No?* Flustered, I explained my presence. Angel was being very kind and sympathetic. Of *course* I could come in, *do* come in out of that weather. Across the threshold, shake the snow out of my eyes, and ...

Inside. Wall-to-wall carpeting, blond-on-blond furniture in a color-TVed living room—Angel explained that, yes, much of the furniture I see belonged to the Zimmermans'—a dining room with a nice old table, a big kitchen sporting all the latest appliances, and ... Bob's breakfast nook! an Archie booth scroll-sawed into Hansel and Gretel Bavarian-American.

Angel informed me that she and her family had just recently moved in. The Marolts were buying the house from Mrs. Zimmerman. The decision to sell had been a tough one for her to make. Bob had offered to take the house and keep it up in case he ever wanted to come back to Hibbing, but Mrs. Zimmerman had said no ... and finally convinced Bob and David that letting the house go was for the best. Bob then, apparently, had said OK, but who are you going to sell it to? Who in Hibbing do you think will be able to afford that house? Old people, right? Old people with top-price pocketbooks and no life in their hats. Not if Bob can help it. Find out what top price is for the house, then cut that price down to struggling-young-couple size and Bob will make up the difference. Doesn't want anyone but young people living in his house. Young people with kids.

Typical of Bob, Angel said. Though she'd never met him. But Angel had heard so much about Bob from Mrs. Zimmerman that she felt as if he practically still lived here. And the basement recreation room, for instance. Mrs. Zimmerman's Bob Dylan Pop Center. Would I like to see? . . .

Mrs. Zimmerman took down most of the posters and things before she moved out, Angel continued, but she hadn't carted them away yet. There were still a few hanging. On the blond pine walls of the rec room—a small wooden affair boxed into one corner of a basement already crowded with humming, rumbling appliances—and they were publicity stills from Bob's movie, personality posters, and dust jackets to his records. In one corner, however, there was a huge pile of stuff: pictures, posters, clippings, Dylan propaganda from around the world. There were photographs, *color* photographs with French or German captions that few people in this country could have seen. Obviously posed publicity shots of Bob in English three-piece suits, Pierre Cardin pastel shirts, and Carnaby Street ties. One in particular was a color photograph of Bob from a French magazine. It showed our impeccably attired 2425 East Seventh Avenue hero seated for lunch at a sidewalk café. He was coldly staring down his photographer from behind a shrimp fork stabbed into a lemon. The caption, roughly translated, read: "Bob Dylan—American pop idol, etc., etc., confesses to reporters that 'My past is so complicated you wouldn't believe it even if I told you.'"

And there had been more junk, too, Angel told me, things like clothes, teddy bears, shoes, and athletic equipment. Mrs. Zimmerman threw most of that out. Boy, though, didn't Angel bet Bob's fans would have had a field day in that stuff. Teddy bears! Angel saved some of the clothes for her kids, but the rest were long gone. Too bad more things weren't salvaged, but what could she do with Mrs. Zimmerman standing right there and...but wait! Here was something...this pair of ice skates! Angel had forgotten she'd snuck them out of the trash. For her little boy. The skates were still in excellent condition, and it really had seemed silly to throw them out. Black figure skates, the blades still sharp...looked like they'd hardly been used. Guess little Bobby didn't spend a whole lot of time ice-skating....

Bob Dylan's *ice skates?*

Back upstairs, Angel was on the telephone calling people Bob's age who might have known him in Hibbing. She got names of fellows who at one time or another were in Bob's band: Chuck Nara, Bill Marinac, and Larry Fabbro. But all three had long since left Hibbing. Angel also found names of some people a little older or younger who might remember Bob. People still in town...and the name of a girl Bob used to go with; the *only* girl anybody seems to remember Bob sticking with for very long. A saucy little blond number, Angel said. Down in Minneapolis now. A Swedish girl, Echo Helstrom.

I spoke with one woman at Angel's (on Bob's old kitchen phone) who remembered him very well. In fact, he had once come over to her house on his motorcycle, to see if maybe she'd like to go for a ride. She'd gotten on only after much coaxing, and well, finally, Bob blasted out of the driveway. But when he turned up Howard Street she made him let her off. She couldn't parade right through the *center of town* that way! After all, nice girls didn't ride on motorcycles.

I asked Angel if there was anything else left in the house reminiscent of Bob. Well, uh, yes. The original bedroom furniture upstairs in Bob and David's room. Would, could?...Sure, why not, I'd seen everything else, might as well take the entire tour. After all, Mrs. Zimmerman had warned Angel this sort of thing might happen.

On the way upstairs, Angel pointed out a little second-story sundeck guard-railed onto the roof of the garage. It was at the very rear of the house and used to be one of Bob's favorite spots. Neighbors have told Angel that in recent years the only way anyone would know Bob was in town was if they saw him sitting there on that porch. Sunning himself, his feet up on the railing, surveying the scene, and. . . .

Angel had kept Bob's room the same for more than just practical reasons. Apparently one of the semiformal conditions of the sale was that Bob could stay at the Marolts in his old room whenever he wished to visit Hibbing. (Mrs. Zimmerman, when she finishes traveling, is to move in with one of Bob's Hibbing-based aunts.) Bob and David's room is across the hall from two larger bedrooms, the master bedroom and another where the boys' grandmother had lived. The boys' room — Bob's *bedroom,* for godsake — looked cramped. There were two single beds perpendicularly set up, a chair, and an old pine dresser. With cigarette burns left by the careless hand of our man himself. I tried out Bob's bed, bouncing on it gingerly. The view from his window in the cold afternoon was bleak. Angel Marolt was rambling on, about Mrs. Zimmerman and her furs, Mrs. Zimmerman and her diamonds, Mrs. Zimmerman and her Cadillac. But I was only half listening. Outside, the snow was swirling back and forth, steaming up the window. An occasional car passed by — a '56 Chevy, a '49 Ford. There was music playing — Hank Williams, Carl Perkins, Elvis, or Gene Vincent — from an old Victrola in the corner. Smoke from cigarettes forbidden to use curled over the dresser, tried to hide in the closet. A stray foot kicked a beat-up guitar sticking out from under the bed. Struck a hollow unfingered chord. Bedspreads, school books, curtain rods, and warm socks. Blue jeans, black loafers, Bible stories, and Bo Diddley — playing loud from the corner now. Over chains through new snow in the street.

TEN GUSH: *Dim Lights, Thick Smoke ...*

Thursday's a big night in Hibbing, for the pre-piano-bar set, that is. Young singles working around town, students from the Junior State College of Hibbing, and vagabonds like me. We were crowded into either the Garden or the Corner lounges, rocking to the sounds of *live* music. Thursday's the night. Only night during the week both bars have bands.

I was enjoying my fourth or fifth Grain Belt Premium while squeezed into a corner booth off the dance floor of the Garden Lounge. People were jitterbugging and twisting. There was an occasional frug, but even that looked hard to get into with the music being played. Blue-Velvet-Ventures, late-fifties-triple-twang. Syrup rock. By a red-blazered, tab-collared quartet that ... entertained requests! But don't worry, I'd already asked. Know no Bob.

Know no Bob. That seemed the slogan of the week. Plenty of people remembered Bobby Zimmerman, probably two or three right here in the Garden Lounge. But Bobby Die-lan? Sure, they've heard of him, and most likely go for his music Muzak style. Or if they were really intellectual like B. J. Rolfzen, listened to his songs recited on record by Sebastian Cabot.

But it had been a long day. Thank goodness for scrapbooking motherhood. And helpful Angel Marolt. I'd finally gotten hold of Melvin Edelstein, too—one of Bob's cousins and manager of Hibbing's two movie theaters. Melvin Edelstein had told me the usual,

Bob was a loner as a kid, used to come to the movies an awful lot...
by himself, mostly. Yes, Melvin Edelstein knew of Bob's movie
Don't Look Back. That's correct, the movie had not been shown in
Hibbing. And would not be. Personally, Melvin Edelstein had been
all for a showing, but... Bob's father had seen the film somewhere,
and so had several other out-of-town relatives and... well, there
had been raised eyebrows. What with the embarrassing gossip
about Bob and drugs just beginning to die down in social Hibbing,
the family had decided against a hometown run. The film had been
scheduled to play in Duluth... but somehow that had never come
to pass either. Yes, Melvin Edelstein had seen Bob at the funeral.
He had looked fit; and, as a matter of fact, Melvin Edelstein had
raised the question of a possible Hibbing showing for *Don't Look
Back*. But Bob himself had been against the idea. People in Hibbing he feared... just wouldn't understand.

I'd called Echo Helstrom's home, too. I'd spoken with her father,
Matt Helstrom, a gruff voice with a throatful of the old country
still hanging on. He didn't know Echo's Minneapolis phone number offhand, but he promised he'd have Mrs. Helstrom call me at
the Androy. Which she did—an enthusiastic lady with happy ya's
and well wishes for whatever I planned to write. She gave me two
numbers, Echo at work and Echo at home. I should call Echo as
soon as possible though, so I wouldn't miss her over the weekend.

A side trip to Minneapolis was becoming more of a necessity. I
actually had enough now for a story, but... I'd reached David
Zimmerman in Minneapolis and he'd agreed to see me. Dylan's
brother! That had been traumatic, finding him. I'd gotten David's
number from his brand-new mother-in-law (telling her I needed
to get in touch with him on business, and had called him a mere
two hours ago. He'd been out at a class, but I called back and...
incredible, he sounded just like Bob. If I hadn't known it was
David I'd have thought I was speaking with the big fella himself.
At first David simply reiterated what Bob's aunt had said, that the
family never granted interviews without consulting Bob, but my
obvious antiestablishmentarian approach and insistent enthusiasm
to meet him overrode all that, and he agreed to see me Friday

night. I assured him that I'd read the liner poetry to *The Times They Are A-Changin'* and that I had no desire to "expose" Bob, and he mumbled hmm and asked me if I was sleeping in my car or if I represented any paper, and I confessed no to both, losing my voice in the process . . . my frigging north country cold.

But that was set up, and I had the number of this girl Echo, so what the hell. Maybe she was the "Girl from the North Country." Fat chance; but there *was* Dylan's brother and just *meeting* him had to be worth the four-hour trip. God knows what he would be like . . . growing up Bobby Die-lan's little brother must do something to your skull. Maybe he'd invite me to stay at his place. Maybe Bob would be there.

I'd moved up the street to the Corner Lounge, much more of what I'd imagined a Hibbing saloon to be like. All the way up at the northwest end of Howard Street, the Corner Lounge is close to the mines . . . in both geography and spirit. A long wooden bar *still* stand-up to a heavy brass rail, spittoons for refuse, and a rockabilly band for sweatin' the red ore dust out of your pores. Timelessly skull-crack, and a perfect place to kiss New Hibbing good-bye.

"Yes sir, lemme have one of those Grain Belts. I'm headin' down the road tomorrow, goin' to Minneapolis. Try to locate a girl name of Echo. Used to run with Bobby Zimmerman. That's right, Bobby Die-lan. Doin' a story on him and Hibbing. Gonna relocate you mothers on the map. Give the Chamber of Commerce a kick in the ass. Next time I'm up this way you'll be peddlin' Bobby Die-lan kewpie dolls and celebratin' Bobby Die-lan Day 8½ times a year. Your kids will be wantin' Bobby Die-lan cowboy outfits for Christmas, and whistlin' 'Home on the Range' through new improved Bobby Die-lan mouth organs. What? Sure I know his brother David's down in Minneapolis. Damn straight, I'm gonna see him. But you better believe I'm fixin' to track down this little split-tail Echo first. No, dammit, lemme buy *you* one. People in this town just won't let a man pay for a drink. Got my eye on that fine young thing you got workin' on stage here, too. . . . She somethin' else? Let's ease over and . . . *looky here* now friend, no need to shove! . . . Ask her if she knows any songs by Bobby Die-lan. Go on, lean up there and just ask. You...she does! What... 'Blowin' in the Wind,' Good Lord, Hibbing, Minnesota's international all-time favorite. No, now don't get bothered, honey, *sure* I want you to play it. *Please* go on and play it, you're the only one that's able. But I'm beggin' you just...dish it up good and country for me sweetheart 'cause that's how both me and my man like to hear it."

ELEVEN GUSH: 'Chinery

But there were a few things I wanted to do before leaving town. Bob had had an old Harley Davidson motorcycle, I'd heard that from somebody, and there was a Harley Davidson dealer out on Highway 37. I'd passed it on my way into Hibbing the first day. The snow had turned to rain in the night, but not even rain actually, just a depressing mist. The Hibbing Harley Davidson dealership sat like a rectangular green sponge in a fully puddled drive as I pulled up. Partially assembled motorcycles clustered in heaps or strained against their half-immersed kickstands. Tarpaulins flapped. I hustled inside.

A big fellow in coveralls and a Powr-House Blue Denim Engineer's cap was bent over in one corner, replacing the chain of a well-ridden BSA. He was the only other person in the shop. I stood and watched him take a link out of the chain, feed it onto the back wheel, and tighten up the lug. He had heard me come in but hadn't bothered to turn around. His work area was filled with machinery—acetylene torches, drills, wrenches, parts of motorcycles. Fascinating little shiny things to keep him busy. You couldn't really blame the guy for not being anxious to see me. My presence didn't count much.

He finished what he was doing and eased over to the counter. I introduced myself, told him what I was doing in Hibbing, and asked the usual. No, the mechanic hadn't really known Bob, but he'd worked on his motorcycle once. Over at the Zimmermans'. Apparently Bob's bike wouldn't start, and Mr. Zimmerman had called Mechanic to see if he could come give her a look. Mechanic had fired it up; no, heck no, he didn't remember what had been wrong with it. That was over ten years ago; no, he never saw Bob after that, but he'd heard Bob made it big. Was a singer or something.

I talked a few minutes more with Mechanic about other affairs; how Japanese motorcycles were thicker than flies; how it wasn't like the old days when a cycle buff could depend on his buddies; and how the big Harley 74s such as Bob had ridden were becoming less and less popular. Tiny little pissant bikes you could take to the shopping center and back were what sold these days. I complimented Mechanic on his Powr-House Blue Denim Engineer's cap, and asked where I might find one. He told me Montgomery Ward's used to carry them, but he wasn't sure anymore. I said so long and headed back into town.

I stopped off first at Crippa's, and took a last look. Guitars were stacked along the left wall, racks of old records stood in rows before me, and somebody was buying his kid a ukulele toward the rear of the store. I bought a harmonica rack from Saleslady and left. She stocked them now, you didn't have to order.

Up at Montgomery Ward's, a clerk begrudgingly sold me a Powr-House Blue Denim Engineer's cap, all the while smiling as if she wished I'd stay for tea. That's a funny feeling, and characteristic of Hibbing, to walk into Montgomery Ward's, Woolworth's, or Sears and find not the nameless gray faces of big-city department store employees, but—veritable Ladies' Auxiliary charmers. Sales personnel are almost always well-dressed, poised-and-polite first citizens of the town. I mean *Bob's mother* worked at Feldman's.

The sun was actually shining when I emerged from Montgomery Ward's. I'd already checked out of the Androy, said good-bye to everyone over there; and felt like taking a few more pictures. I drove by Zimmerman's Furniture and Electric, past Bus Andy's Conoco station, over to Seventh Avenue past the high school . . . to Bob's old house. My new hat felt warm and snappy as I stood across the street taking pictures. Not like before in the sleet and rain. I should have had that hat a long time ago. I crossed the street and

climbed the steps on up to the door. Sure would like to have a picture of Bob's ice skates. Who would believe that? I could put them
out here on the top step . . . but no answer. Angel's big black Thunderbird wasn't in the driveway, either. Nobody was home. I walked
back around to the backyard and took several shots of Bob's bedroom window. Who would believe *that?* And the garage where
maybe he used to practice with his band. And B. J. Rolfzen's pink
cottage. And a street sign and a mailbox.

MACROGUSH *

Barreling down Highway 61 away from Duluth and the frustration of several futile telephone calls, I was headed south to Minneapolis at last. South to Echo Helstrom, David Zimmerman, and the University of Minnesota—Bob's freshman year amusement park. Remember all that impressive rant on the back of Bob's first album—about flunking out after six months but getting a lot of reading done nevertheless; staying up all night plowing through the philosophy of Kant instead of *Living with the Birds* for a science class or something... But Highway 61—roaring out of Lake Superior's industrial southland, cutting a swath through East Minnesota's hunting and fishing territory, over rivers with names like Kettle and Willow, big choppy lakes like Sturgeon and Moosehead, past northwoods towns like Mahtowa, Sandstone, and Pine City... The entire countryside blindingly bright in the loudest of red and yellow falls. Colors intensified by reflections in shoeshine black water. The sky once again wide open to cloudless blue infinity, and not another car on the bare midafternoon highway.

For experiment's sake I kept fooling with the radio, trying everything—A.M., F.M., even shortwave. But couldn't pick up much. Local reports on hunting and fishing, some Lawrence Welk—super-

---

* Now please cue up either side one, band two of *The Freewheelin' Bob Dylan* or side one, band one of *Nashville Skyline.*

market swing, and an occasional forest ranger. Pretty soon though, I was getting top-forty stations from the Twin Cities area, civilization was sprouting up, Bee Gees were wailing "gotta get a message to yew," and before I knew it I was beneath the golden arches of a Minneapolis McDonalds' drive-in.

I found a telephone and called the number Echo's mother had given me, Echo-at-work, the office of a Minneapolis film company. A voice answered promptly. It was Echo's.

"Oh *yes*, I was expecting your call. But another five minutes and you would have missed me. Now hold on, you don't have to go through all that. I've heard everything about you. My mother telephoned and told me you were doing a story on Bob. Of course you can see me, but it'll have to be at my place which is a mess, and I hope you don't mind making it pretty soon 'cause I have to drive up to Hibbing tonight..." and on and on in the most intriguing voice I'd heard since arriving in the north country. Saucy was the word.

I had about fifteen minutes to kill before I could meet Echo, so I started tracking down David Zimmerman. He'd given me three numbers where I should be able to reach him: his apartment, his office, and the scene of a rehearsal he was to attend that evening. David was a student at the University of Minnesota, seeking a degree in music education. But as that September sixth column from the Hibbing *Daily Tribune* read (the one Bert Ackerson had given me back in Hibbing), quoting from a Sunday supplement article in the Minneapolis *Tribune*, "at the age of 22 David is 'eking out a fairly good career discovering, managing, teaching, and working with young performers.' He's very candid about the 'indispensable in,' that the fact he's brother to folk-rock hero Bob Dylan 'initially opened a lot of doors at Columbia' for him." An undergraduate A and R man I suppose one might call David . . . with "high office relations" on the Board of Governors.

Caught David at the first number I tried, but there was confusion as to where and when we should meet, and the hint of apprehension in David's voice at the mention of my appointment with Echo, a chaos of thwarted plans steadily building . . . until David gave me another number where he'd be until nine thirty at least, call him before then if I got the chance.

Off through the unfamiliar streets of Minneapolis, Echo's directions in my head, telepathic rays drawing me to Echo's basement apartment. Down a short flight of cement steps, past washer-dryer central to bungalow number four. A simple tap on the door, and . . .

Echo—blue eyes, Swedish long-blond hair, black and white houndstooth outfit, skirt way up above knee-high black patent leather boots—plus the finest smile this side of White Bear Lake!

Echo ushered me into a laundry-cluttered living room, shoved a stack of Sunday newspapers off the couch, and invited me to sit down. She sounded less sure of herself here than on the phone, but kept up a steady flow of conversation, all about having spoken with her mother this afternoon, how excited she had been that a *writer* wanted to interview *her* daughter . . . and it wasn't long before Echo settled into a more relaxed state, the smile really came on, and she was remembering times with Bob:

"First place I ever *saw* him was at ice-skating, I think. We were about twelve or thirteen, and he called me over to peek through a knothole at his fingers. He was walking them up and down a bench like little legs. Who could forget anything somebody would do that was that weird! Bob was already playing funny games. But first place I actually *met* him I guess was over at the L & B Café in Hibbing. That was back at the beginning of our eleventh-grade year, 1957 I think. I'd seen Bob around school before, but he'd never really spoken to me since that time at ice-skating. He was always so well dressed and quiet, I had him pegged for a goody-goody. You know, one of those kids who never wanted to have any fun; always going to church and listening to their parents, you know. Well, that's the way I figured Bob was.

"We were sitting in the L & B that night, my girlfriend and me, when Bob came over. I'd seen him only a few minutes before, outside in the street, and you'd never guess what he was doing. He was standing right out in the middle of the sidewalk, playing his guitar and singing! Right in front of the Moose Lodge, all by himself . . . but when he came into the L & B he was with some friends, and they just came over and sat down. I suppose you could say they were trying to pick us up, but I don't know. Bob still looked so innocent and well scrubbed I never even thought about that.

"We talked for a while about nothing in particular and had another Coke I suppose—I used to have chocolate-orange or cherry Cokes, yum!—'till I thought of asking him what seemed to me a pretty stupid question at the time, you know, just conversation. He'd just finished telling me about how he played the piano as well as the guitar, and was forming a band with some of his friends, local kids, when the name of a song I'd heard the night before popped into my head. The only rock and roll music you could get in Hibbing in those days was broadcast late at night over a colored station from Little Rock, Arkansas.* A girlfriend and I listened to it every night, but I never would have thought Bob did. I guess I mentioned the name of that song really just to show him how much *he* knew about music. Anyway, the song was 'Maybelline' and it was brand new to me.

"'"Maybelline,"' he said. '"Maybelline" by *Chuck Berry?* You bet, I've heard it! . . .' And on and on about Chuck Berry, Fats Domino, Little Richard, Jimmy Reed—Bob thought he was fabulous, the best!—and everybody who was popular those days in other parts of the country, but who might as well have not even existed as far as most of Hibbing was concerned. He kept going on about their music and how great it was, how he loved to play it himself, and how someday he wanted more than anything else to be a rock and roll singer—all with his eyes sort of rolled up in his head, in a whole different *world* until . . . it finally dawned on him. He stopped what he was saying, leaned halfway across the table, his eyes great big, and whispered, 'You . . . you don't mean that you too . . . *you* listen to Gatemouth Page out of Shreveport? I said yes *I* did, had been for two years, and just how long had he thought *he* was so special being a fan of Gatemouth's!

* and Shreveport, Louisiana.

"Well, that did the trick. We talked about music and how he wanted so much to be a singer, about movies, actors, and actresses . . . and I even told him how I was planning on being a movie star, which he really got excited about, promising he could get me into all the movies that came to town free because his uncle owned the big theater. We kept talking about how great show business was, and how someday we'd sure surprise everyone in Hibbing, until the L & B's closing time. But Bob wasn't anywhere near ready to stop then, so he said, 'Come on, follow me!' and led the four of us upstairs over the dining room where he said there was a piano. The door was locked and I picked it with my penknife, but we were too scared to go in. Bob went in by himself and played for a while though, but he finally got scared, too. As we were sneaking back downstairs he asked if he could meet me after school the next day. . . so I could come over to his house and hear him perform. I said yeah sure I wanted to, 'cause he'd surprised me all right and I no longer thought he was a goody-goody. . . . Still, now that I think back, it was a whole month before he kissed me."

Echo laughed at this, looking at me for the first time since she'd started talking about Bob. I hadn't had to ask any questions. And she'd hardly moved, wasn't fidgeting at all. She'd just tucked her legs up under her on the couch. But her facial expressions had been going like gangbusters. Echo was a good actress, and storyteller—with a trace of tongue-in-cheek at the rough edges of her tale. But not for me, for someone out there across the room somewhere.

"I wasn't sure whether his family liked me or not," Echo continued, "once I became sort of a fixture around the house and they realized I'd turned into more than just Bob's little friend from school. I don't know if it was 'cause I was from the wrong side of town or wasn't Jewish or what. They were always nice to me, but I could tell something was funny. Like Bob would act strange in a lot of ways. He used to make me go into his uncle's movie theater alone, for instance, and then he'd sneak in and join me. I didn't even think about Bob being *Jewish* 'til quite a while after we'd met, 'cause I never cared about things like that anyhow. And I only asked him about it once. There was another fellow, John Bucklen, who used to pal around with Bob and me. The three of us, we were always doing things together. John wanted to be a disc jockey, that was going to be his claim to fame. He is too, up in St. Cloud; and I'm a booker for a film company, not an *actress* like I used to dream about, but close enough; and of course, Bob is Bob. We all three actually made it, see! Anyway, one night—I guess it was that first night, while I was picking the lock upstairs at the Moose Lodge— John was there, and I casually said to Bob, 'Gee, *Zimmerman*, that's a funny name. Is it Jewish?' Well, Bob didn't answer anything at *all*, he just looked straight ahead with his face sort of funny. Later in the week John took me aside at school and said, 'Listen Echo, don't ever ask about Bob being Jewish again. He doesn't like to talk about it.' Gosh, I hadn't meant to upset him, I was only interested! It was that same year, eleventh grade, that Bob came over to my house after school one day and told me he'd finally decided on his stage name. Yes, it was 'Dylan'... after that poet, I think."

Echo excused herself for a moment, and I had a chance to catch my breath. And I almost hadn't come down to Minneapolis! No one had *ever* heard anything like this!... Or had they? I'd better make sure. I helped myself to some stale peanuts from the coffee table and looked around the living room. Typical stuff, a record player at one end of the couch with about twenty albums, a huge old television in the center of the room, dinette furniture, some anonymous prints, family-style photographs, an ironing board... no pictures or posters of Bob, though. I was just leaning down toward the stack of records when Echo reemerged from the back of the apartment, barefoot, and in a different outfit.

"Have you ever talked to other writers about any of this?" I blurted through a mouthful of peanuts.

She strolled over to the record player and flicked it on—Tom Jones. "Yes, a man called me from Hibbing last May to ask if he could see me. A reporter from New York... Robert Shelton. Bob had given him my name 'cause he was doing a book on Bob or something, and was coming out to Hibbing. I talked to him and his wife for a long time, but they had a tape recorder and I couldn't concentrate hardly at all."

"Did he say when his book would be out? He's doing an authorized study of Bob, apparently. And he'd already talked to a bunch of the people I tracked down in Hibbing. Must have had some names before he went out, I guess."

"Well, Mr. Shelton told me he'd gotten my name from Bob—as somebody he'd known real well in Hibbing. That's all Mr. Shelton said, he didn't mention anything about when his book was going to come out."

"That doesn't matter now, anyway. Let's get back to Bob, OK? Exactly when and for how long did you all go together? What was the year?"

"We went steady that whole eleventh-grade year. A winter and a summer—1957–1958, I think. Bob was pretty serious about his band and they practiced a lot. It was all a blues sound then, what we heard on the radio. Bob sang and played the piano, and he used to practice with the band in garages around the neighborhood. Nobody liked their music much, least of all Bob's voice. I used to get so upset, for days ahead of time when I knew he was going to sing in public. He and the band played around town fairly often, at school assemblies, at the youth club, and at Collier's Barbecue. At Collier's it wasn't so bad, we'd be there on a Saturday afternoon with friends or something, and that could be wonderful. But in the big auditoriums people would laugh and hoot at Bob, and I'd just sit there embarrassed, almost crying. One time in particular, I remember the band was scheduled to play over at school. I was nervous as usual, standing around waiting for them to come on. But finally they did, and I shut my eyes and put my fingers in my ears like always. They were so loud! And I didn't want to see or hear people laughing. Well the band started, and I was standing there like that praying everything would be all right when the girl next to me pulled my hands away from my face and screamed, 'Listen!' At first I couldn't hear anything but the band. Bob *always* had the amplifiers too high, it was practically impossible to hear his voice. They were doing a Ray Charles sort of boogie, *really* loud . . . but gradually it got so I could distinguish Bob's voice, and you know what he was singing? He was *howling* over and over again, 'I gotta girl and her name is Echo!' making up verses as he went along. I guess that was the first song I'd ever heard him sing that wasn't written by somebody else. And it was about me! People laughed at Bob that night like always, but I didn't even care."

"Was that the Jacket Jamboree Talent Festival, where someone told me he broke a foot pedal on the piano?"

"Right! I think he kinda got in trouble with the music department for that, too."

"Was he upset when he came off, you know, that people laughed at him?"

"Oh, no! I saw him right after, and he was really proud! He had asked me to meet him outside after the performance . . . it took him weeks to talk me into that, because, well one just doesn't get up in school and walk out you know . . . but he finally convinced me it was all right. So I did, like a stupe, and we didn't get caught. Bob just walked me around in the cool evening air, asking over and over, 'Didja like it? Didja like it?' He told me what he'd been singing then, too. He was as big-eyed and excited as ever. I guess Bob lived in his own world, 'cause apparently the audience's booing and laughter hadn't bothered him in the least.

"Bob was such a dreamer, anyhow. We talked about each other's careers a lot, how someday we'd really show people in Hibbing. Boy, neither one of us could wait to get out of that town. There was really *nothing* in Hibbing either of us cared about—except each other. Oh, we were really in love. Everybody laughs at kids when they fall in love, saying how they don't know what it means or anything, but that's not true. Kids know. We'd talk about getting married a lot, just to get out of Hibbing for one thing, but Bob always said no, we can't even think about that. Would interfere with our careers. It was always the career first with Bob. I thought about a career a lot too, sure, but with Bob it was an obsession. He really wanted to show everybody . . . and he has, I guess. Though few people in Hibbing could even care."

Echo paused here a second, slowly smoothing out her skirt. She was still staring way off across the living room. I ventured another question: "What about some of Bob's later songs—the ones that don't specifically mention Hibbing, but sort of sound like they might have Hibbing in mind. Can you think of any like that offhand?"

"Yes...that song 'Positively 4th Street.' I remember when it came out I said to myself, Bob wrote that song about Hibbing. For all those people who used to boo him when he played, and who probably now couldn't be nicer or more polite when they see him. Some of those people up there were just awful to us. I'm glad he wrote that song, I really laughed when I heard it.

"We had some good times together though, up there. Bob was always so crazy! He'd imagine the nuttiest things, and then we'd have to act them out. He kept quiet most of the time, but when he got an idea his eyes would get *great* big and you couldn't stop him talking until he'd finished telling you everything about it. He was all the time making things out to be more serious than they were, too. Like I remember once after school we were up in Bob's room listening to records or something, and nobody else was home. I wasn't supposed to be allowed upstairs, you see. Well all of a sudden the front door slams and Bob gets really scared. Actually, I don't know now if he was scared so much as he saw the whole situation as an opportunity to do something crazy, and was just excited. Anyway, his eyes got all big and he whispered, 'My grandmother's home, we can't let her find us up here alone!' He'd have to do something. So he put me in the closet and told me to wait and *not move* until I heard him go outside, and then climb out the window and he'd catch me. He gathered up all his schoolbooks and went downstairs to tell his grandmother he had to go to the library. Then he came back up and snuck me out onto the sunporch, went down to tell his grandmother good-bye, slammed the front door, and snuck around the side of the house to catch me coming off the porch. His plan worked somehow, and he was so proud! But Bob was awful silly about things like that. I mean, sure, his grandmother didn't find us, but there I was in broad daylight, hanging off of Bob's second-story sunporch, my skirt up around my waist, with Bob down below waiting to catch me, and I guess everybody in the whole *neighborhood* saw that!

"But we didn't care. I suppose I was just as crazy as Bob to go along with some of those things, and enjoyed them as much too. We had our fights though. I remember one time we'd had a big one, over at my house, and my mother and father had gotten into it. Everybody was mad, and I didn't see Bob for a couple of days. 'Til one afternoon I was sitting in the living room doing something or other with my parents, and the doorbell rang. I got up to answer it and thought I heard music, but didn't even think until I opened the door... and there was Bob, decked out in one of those TV gambler's vests he used to wear, beating on his guitar and singing, 'Do you want to dance and hold my hand?'... you remember the Bobby Freeman song that was popular then. Anyhow, boy was I surprised! He stood there on the doorstep and sang it all the way through once, then pushed past me into the living room and sang it again for my parents. Then he just wouldn't stop, but paraded around the house singing that song 'til all of us were laughing so hard we'd forgotten what the fight was even about."

Echo was going strong again, and I wasn't about to stop her, couldn't have if I'd wanted to. I just sat there with my mouth open.

"Bob was always—how would you say it without sounding corny—I don't know, 'looking around.' For *anything* different, but mostly things he thought would help him in his music. Like Negroes—no, 'colored people,' he insisted on calling them that, and to this day I practically always say 'colored.' You know, there aren't any colored people in Hibbing? Even today! That used to make Bob just furious. He loved their music so much, everytime he'd hear about one coming through town he'd go and find him just to meet him and talk to him and find out what he was like. That probably sounds funny to you, but it was *really* funny, not funny but *strange* for us to see one of those people. Bob would all the time drag me along, too. I remember one day we had to drive way over to Virginia—that's a town out on the Range—just to see this one colored fellow who was disc jockey on the radio station over there, and who was from the South I think. Anyway, he and his wife got to be pretty good friends with Bob and me.

"Traveling started to become important for Bob, too, and I suppose that's one of the big reasons we broke up. He began taking off every weekend, going down to Minneapolis or St. Paul to listen to music he said, but I knew he was seeing other girls as well. That didn't bother me so much as just being left alone all the time. This went on for a couple of months I guess before I finally couldn't stand it any longer and got up enough nerve to give him back his I.D. bracelet. Was right after one of those lonely weekends . . . on a Monday morning. I knew I'd see Bob in the hall at school, so I decided to give him his bracelet back then. I spotted him strutting through the crowd with a couple of his friends in tow, all full of show business and image and telling tales of gosh knows what had gone on down in Minneapolis that weekend. I just walked right up to him and told him I had something to say, and handed him back his I.D. bracelet. His first reaction was to push me over against the lockers and whisper real loud, 'Shh . . . not *here!*' His eyes were all big, but I don't think he really took me seriously until later. I didn't see him all day, after school or anything, but that night he came over to my house. He was crying, and wanted to know what I thought I was doing. I went out to his car with him and we talked for a while, but he wouldn't listen. I kept telling him over and over that it wouldn't work his way; finally I had to jump out of the car and run inside. That was one of the hardest things I've ever done. Oh, it's silly I guess . . . but just think: If I had been a fink and made up, Bob might be in Hibbing selling appliances right now, and the world wouldn't have him.

"After that, I didn't see him for a good long while. He went out with some other girls, and I had plenty of dates too . . . but neither one of us ever went steady again. I didn't have much to do with him in the twelfth grade; he was always in Minneapolis on weekends and I avoided him in school. He wrote a page-long sort of letter-poem to me in my yearbook at the end of the eleventh grade . . ."

"Do you have that *here?*"

"No, it's up in Hibbing at my mother's. But anyhow, after graduation and that next summer I didn't see Bob until Minneapolis. I'd moved down here, and he was a freshman at the University. He was living in a fraternity house off campus, and we went out together a few times . . . but he was getting into the beatnik business, with the coffee house and everything, and I gradually stopped seeing him. I moved into Dinkytown—that's the student section here—mostly because he wanted me to, but the parties I didn't like much 'cause everyone was sort of . . . well, degenerate. Like he called me once right before he quit school and invited me to this party where he said there was free food, free wine, free love, and all the girls were sitting around with no blouses on. I drew the line at that! And don't guess I saw him again 'til he came back from New York a year or so later.

"He'd just recorded his first album and was in Minneapolis for a concert at the university. He called me and asked if I'd meet him downtown, and we'd go to a party. I said OK, 'cause I hadn't seen him for so long or anything. He'd changed a lot. He was skinny, whereas he'd always been sort of chubby. He had on blue jeans and a workshirt and was . . . *dirty*. We met in front of Penney's, and he gave me a copy of his album and bought me a Coke at Woolworth's. I was kind of embarrassed, 'cause he'd told me we were going to a party and all, and I had on a nice white dress and little white gloves. . . . But we walked together all the way across Third Avenue bridge and over into southeast, holding hands and talking—me with my white dress and him in his boots and blue jeans.

"I asked him about New York and the music he was playing, too, and whatever had happened to the hard blues stuff? He said, 'Oh don't worry it's still there, but folk music is what's really going to be big,' and that's how he was going to make it. I told him I didn't like the sound of it as well as the other stuff, and he said, 'I know, but this is the coming thing.' With his eyes all big. He played his guitar and harmonica and songs from his album at the party that night, and everybody loved it. Bob was happy in the limelight again like old times, I could see that, only now people didn't seem to laugh at him. We both got pretty tipsy and later when we were alone he got very sentimental and asked me to come back to New York with him, and he'd get me an apartment and we could be together again. I started crying and telling him no, but he kept talking about it until finally I got mad and said, 'Well what about this folksinger Joan Baez you're supposed to be in love with, just what about her?' Bob didn't say anything, but got up and walked across the room to his suitcase. He pulled out a framed photograph, came back over, and shoved it in front of me. It was Joan Baez. 'Do you see this!' he said. 'Do you see it? Do you think I could ever fall in love with a face like that?' Well I really started crying then, and got sort of hysterical and ran down the stairs and out of the house, and walked all the way home. I still knew it wouldn't work. That was the last time I saw Bob ... though he's called me just to say hello since then. Since he's really become famous. Once or twice."

Echo was sitting quietly again, toying with a strand of hair. I asked if she'd ever heard that song "Girl from the North Country."

"Yes, that's on Bob's second album, isn't it?"

"Uh-huh. Do you think it's about you?"

Echo was silent for a moment. "Sure, I like to think it's about me. I *know* it's about me, there's no one else it could be about. And even if there was ... no, it's about me. Bob never wrote me a letter to *tell* me it was about me or anything, but ... then that would have been kind of silly, wouldn't it? And besides, he knew he didn't have to."

There was a sudden knock at the door. Echo jumped—but got up to answer it. Her nephew, come to pick her up for the weekend jaunt to Hibbing. Echo introduced me and hurriedly explained my presence while packing a few things for her trip. Echo's nephew had been just a little boy when Bob was still around. He remembered Bob sitting on the edge of his bed, playing the guitar. But that was about all. Echo's nephew didn't say much—and Echo didn't have much more to say either. Except that she was sorry she had to rush off. I told her don't be silly, she'd been incredibly helpful and more than kind to allow me so much of her time ... and that I understood perfectly. It was a long way back up to Hibbing.

TWELVE GUSH: *Ric's a Blues Guitar Player...*

I drove straight to the first bar I could find on Central Avenue and had a beer. Nasty place, dirty, with a pool table and hostile working types clustered about, drunk two hours after getting off the job. But I didn't care. In the midst of sculpted crewcuts and the heavy butts of pool cues—faces around me frozen into snarls—I tried to put it all back together. ECHO, scribbled into my little blue notebook, ECHO and everything she'd said. ECHO and Bob doing this, ECHO and someone else, someplace... but *Echo*, the "Girl from the North Country"... A prince among Dylan buffs, I quaffed the dregs of my Grain Belt Premium and ordered another.

But I still had to call David Zimmerman—Dylan's brother and Dylan's girl on the same day. The Black Angel in me wept.

Reached David at his rehearsal, and after much hassle concerning directions and what place would be easiest for me to find, he decided on a downtown bar called Duff's, meet him there at ten. Fine, I had a couple of hours yet, and could maybe do some sightseeing. While I was still in the phone booth though, I figured I'd try to call this fellow John Bucklen. Got through to St. Cloud information and was given a number—but turned out to be some guy with the same name who ran a very loud and unsympathetic tavern, and who had never heard of *Bob Dylan* or *Bobby Zimmerman* or anybody. So...

To kill time, I headed down by the University of Minnesota campus, to try to get an idea of what it was like. I passed a row of fraternity houses, maybe the one Bob lived in, but I didn't stop. I was really looking for the Ten O'Clock Scholar, the Minneapolis coffee house where Bob used to hang out and perform. It was in the student quarter called Dinkytown, but I couldn't seem to find it. I asked a policeman, who informed me that the old Scholar had been replaced by a new Scholar in another neighborhood. He gave me directions, and after crossing the Mississippi River about nine times, I located Scholar-new. It was red on the outside and in a terrible neighborhood. Right on the corner of a mammoth highway construction site. Inside, it was . . . well, depressingly passé. The fellow running the place, for instance—the same kind of guy who had run coffee houses when I was involved, the guy who couldn't really play, but who had the best guitar . . . no, not even the best, but the most expensive . . . and who knew all about mikes and sound systems and money changing, and could name you the side men on Lightnin' Hopkins' third album if you'd only ask. An indispensable sort, but archetypically sad in his enthusiasm. You'd always catch him practicing. . . .

This fellow remembered Bob, but hadn't known him personally. That was all a little before his time, the old Scholar. He said Tony Glover might be in later though; he knew Bob real well. And a few others of that crowd. I told him thanks anyway and sat down. I could do without Tony Glover—the people already here were starting to give me those protectively hostile looks: don't shake the scene. And Tony Glover was supposed to be a wild man; I was in no mood for that. You're messing with Bob's private life, aincha? Blues singers were notoriously candid. Oh shit, it was all so intertwined, how could you begin to think of those coffee-house days without Dylan? There was no way. You couldn't sit in a place like this for very long without remembering.

In Washington, the Showboat Lounge on Sunday nights when Charlie Byrd was off, and every folkie in town would huddle . . . this was really in the old days now, '61, '62 . . . and the night balladeer Paul Clayton brought in a stranger to perform, a kid like us, but *different*. . . and people wouldn't listen, wouldn't even pay attention to this horny guitar and harmonica stuff—I wasn't there, but legend has it that Bob finally stopped in the middle of a number, banged the mike, and screamed "*Listen,* you mothers, better pay attention *now* 'cause you're gonna be hearing big things from me!" And later, after Bob's first album appeared, our trips to Gerde's Folk City in the Village, and Bob's concerts in Philadelphia, and hearing that he had showed up at the Ontario Place here in town to dig Pat Webb's blues guitar act, and the Martin Luther King march on the steps of the Lincoln Memorial when Bob sang "The Ballad of Medgar Evers" and "Gospel Plow" in duet with Joanie . . . and everybody *who was cool,* dig, carrying their harmonica racks on the outside of their guitar cases—around the handle, next to your hand— and how many Dylan songs do *you* do? laugh at the poor Kingston Trio–type slobs, and did you make Newport last week, catch Dylan working that whip? surly little pecker, isn't he, but did you hear him do "With God on Our Side," what a song. We sang it up and down the East Coast. "Can you give me the lyrics to that, man?" or cats asking for specific verses as an encore when we were done . . . but that was all part of the game, the collector's trip re-upped city style. And the Charlottesville scene at Paul Clayton's cabin—a scene my partner Linn Barnes and I never made, but heard about from Paul at the Showboat—with Bob apparently really getting into riding bicycles around town, up and down the campus, blowing the blue Brooks Brothers button-down set's minds; UVA! and the evening drinking at the Gaslight, but not much 'cause John Tuck, the Gaslight's owner, never got along with Paul very well, but there *had* been music there, what with Carolyn Hester, Dick Farina, Joanie, and god knows who else from the city dropping down . . . and us just sort of *hearing* about all this up in Washington, a little awed, a *little,* christ! and not being able to get into . . . oh, Joe Latham of the Alexandria Folklore Center brought us back reports, "Yeah, Dylan was there," but Joe was on the fringe, too, and. . . .

Well, it petered out some in college, not really petered out but *changed*. . . until the excitement of *Bringin' It All Back Home* and

"Mr. Tambourine Man" with drugs, and that incredibly funny/sad interview in *Playboy,* and *what kind of a pervo has Dylan turned into?* with that cover of *Highway 61,* and so on, gradually learning to understand a little better, never completely, but a few things like "She Belongs to Me" or the skeleton keys of the rain, and getting stoned to "Like a Rolling Stone" and . . .

Well, here I was, in this folk graveyard, watching the eternally fat but oh-so-hip waitress setting up microphones onstage, and the manager is nudging me, just to let me know, you know, *like the show is about to start, man, and it's a dollar fifty cover. . .* so I finished my Peruvian tea and split, I mean I had a date with Dylan's brother, *Dylan's brother!* Oh shit, what that once would have meant.

THIRTEEN GUSH: *I Got a Million Friends*

Found Duff's after a complicated journey through Minneapolis's central shopping district. A futuristic, one-way traffic hang-up impossible to navigate. Glass and steel skyscrapers towering over fountained malls and fifty-foot-wide sidewalks. Captain Videoed corner-bus-stop lounges, heated for your convenience. And everything so *clean...clean...*

Duff's was terrible—some sort of Friday-night singles club, reeking of Joe Namath—everybody resplendent in midwestern-hip, lots of carefully trimmed sideburns and white nylon turtlenecks. Pictures of the Minnesota Twins and Vikings on the walls, heads constantly turning toward the door, secretaries out for a night on the town, young investment counselors there at the gate, brand-new dresses, shoes to match...a strange spot for Bob Dylan's brother to want to meet you for a drink. I'd made the mistake of arriving half an hour early, and David Zimmerman was late.

I was sitting by the door when he finally came in. He was by himself, not with his wife as I'd expected; but we recognized each other from mutual telephone descriptions. David was short like Bob, but stocky. Close to fat. He wore glasses; and well-tailored sports clothes—stylish—jodhpur boots, mod English jacket, and cuffless tapered trousers.

Turned out David's wife Gail was with him after all, but outside, circling the block. Apparently she couldn't get into Duff's with slacks on; the weekend, David explained. He suggested we leave

Duff's and try someplace else, which was swell by me, but on the way out he leaned over and said, "Hey, let's put some people on." Gail pulled up in David's brand-new Buick, and David pretended we were trying to pick her up. "Hows-abouta ride, honey?" We both piled into the front seat—*seats* actually, they were bucket. David and Gail had a good chuckle, but the doorman at Duff's didn't look too put-on.

We stopped at a combination restaurant/fancy motor inn, that had its own parking lot, a key attraction in downtown Minneapolis, but David was worried we wouldn't get in there either—because of Gail's slacks. We did though . . . but on the way, David tried another put-on. At the cashier's counter he paused to grab a toothpick from a little stainless steel dispenser, and spilled about thirty on the floor. As he was bending over to clean up the mess, the cashier said consolingly, "That's okay, people do it all the time." David stood up and said, "Oh really? Well, in that case I don't want to be different"—and left the toothpicks on the floor. The cashier didn't look put-on. Just a little pissed off.

We settled at a table, David with a Bloody Mary and a five-ounce sirloin-hamburger special he wanted to share with Gail. Me with a Budweiser this time, in tune with the classy company I was keeping. Much joking with the waitress; I tried to get into it as best I could, but something was wrong. David was eyeing me in a peculiar way. He seemed friendly, but . . . protective isn't quite the word . . . maybe just nervous. But how could Bob Dylan's *brother* be nervous? He couldn't be scared of *me*, could he?

David was doing a lot of talking, but not saying much. He asked me right off whom I'd seen. I told him, and he tried to discount practically everything they'd said. He told me Angel Marolt's ice-skate story was false. Bob had never skated in his life. The skates had been David's; he and his father had often skated together, but Bob was seldom up for that sort of thing. David had never heard of Bob's babysitter, Don McKenzie (I found out later he was known as "Bud."). And some of the guys I had listed as having been in Bob's band, he told me Bob never knew. You just couldn't trust people when they were talking about celebrities, he said. Not their fault really, but people tend to make things up. I told David that I'd just spent a *very* interesting couple of hours with Echo Helstrom. He had nothing to say about that; pulled on his Bloody Mary instead.

I played back a few of the stories Echo had told me. David's reaction was frightening—silence. So I tried a different tack. I talked about my visit to the high school, and how I'd seen old teachers, heard some great tales, and had a glance at Bob's transcript. What's that?—David bit—Bob's transcript? Who showed it to me? Oh, someone in the office. Who though, the principal? Gosh I don't remember, anyhow I *snuck* a look, he didn't Xerox a copy for me or anything. David was silent. Visions of principals dead in his head.

I asked him about *Don't Look Back*. He told me Bob was dissatisfied with the film—so much so that he had sued D. A. Pennebaker. But had lost. The judge had ruled that if Bob knew some fool was following him around with a camera, he should have at least known enough to watch himself.

David let me in on only a couple more interesting things: I asked about Bob having listened to the Little Rock radio station, hoping at least *that* tale would get an affirmative nod. It did, David said, yes, he could remember Bob doing that. He also remembered the L & B Café and concerts at Collier's. But he wouldn't expound upon anything. I asked if he'd seen the story in a recent *Village Voice* about Bob giving his motorcycle to a gardener . . . no, David said, he hadn't seen that. Though he remembered the gardener—at Albert Grossman's in Woodstock. The gardener was an old guy, and a real loser. I asked if the bike wasn't pretty well smashed up from Bob's accident. David laughed and said, "Know how Bob hurt himself on that motorcycle? He was riding around the backyard on the *grass* and slipped. That's all. The newspapers played it up big. Writers'll do that. They had Bob scarred, blind, an idiot, and half dead." He really didn't break his neck then? I asked. Sure, David said—if a cracked vertebra is a broken neck.

Gail finally yawned. And David announced that it was time to go home. I picked up the check, and faced the silent rage of our put-on cashier. In the car, I asked about Bob back in New York— what sort of music he liked now, the contemporary songwriters he admired ... David had been talking about Leonard Cohen ... but Bob didn't listen to much of anything anymore, apparently. Except country-western. We pulled up across the street from my car. I thanked David and Gail for having met me so late. It was after midnight by now. David shook my hand and said, that's all right but ... just one thing. Watch out when you write your story, man. You mean about Echo? I smile. Yeah, about Echo. Don't turn the whole thing into a "true confessions" piece. You know, just watch the nitty-gritty. Sure David, I know. Good night, as the big Buick drove off. Condensation from dual exhausts trailing him up the street. It was cold, twenty-five to thirty degrees. And I didn't seem to be able to get used to it.

Somewhere in the maze of city blocks between the restaurant and Interstate 94 East, I came across Highway 61. It was weird seeing it again, here in the commercial gut of downtown St. Paul. Nothing but a street—gray, anonymous, and cut up by traffic lights. Highway 61. A long way from the Lake Superior hills— Duluth—and the village of Hibbing.

INTER—MEANTIME—JOUR

CORRESPONDENCE/COMMENTARY *

—*Received the following note* from Echo one week after returning home from Minneapolis. Enclosed was a Xerox copy of the page-long letter-poem Bob wrote in her high school yearbook the day they both finished eleventh grade.

October 11, 1968

Dear Toby,

Hope you can read the parts my mother "censored." You know, I thought of it after I talked to you that Bob might not have liked my talking to you. I didn't even think of it before because I'd talked to the Sheltons and it seemed like it would be okay for me to talk to you. Of course, I'm sure you won't be writing anything malicious about him anyway. I suppose you'll try to meet him and talk to him too, and I would appreciate it very much if you would make sure to ask him if it would be alright to write about anything I told you. Even though I never have anything to do with him anymore, or him with me, I wouldn't want him to get mad at me, just for old time's sake. Okay?

It was a pleasure to meet you and talk to you. I could tell by the way you talked about him that you were very interested and had

---

* Please check the liner notes to *Joan Baez in Concert, Part 2* before starting this section. A 1963 winterlude for Joanie, with good stuff about Hibbing, good philosorap about Bob and his art. Good poem.

spent a lot of time listening to his songs and reading about him. I hope you were able to find John, too.

Maybe I'll hear from you again someday.

Echo

The letter-poem's format is standard "remember when?" but Bob's phrasing already shows characteristic irony and understatement. And he's dropping consonants and vowels... "yo" for "your," "'m" for "them," "ol" for "old." The letter-poem is scribbled in faulty penmanship and smudged from Echo's mother's attempts to crayon out some offensive words. But Bob's schoolboy sentiment remains otherwise intact; the letter-poem reads very much like one of his songs... finishing with the shakily determined flourish: "Well Echo, I better make it, huh—Love to the most beautiful girl in school, Bob—"

October 15, 1968

Dear Echo,

Thanks for your nice note and Bob's letter-poem, god! I never thought you'd actually send it. I've framed it already, and it's hanging on the wall right in front of me... directly over the turntable to my record player. You can't imagine how receiving that blew my mind. I immediately went out and had twenty Xerox copies made, but I'm afraid to send them to any of my friends for fear they'll somehow abuse the privilege. And I don't want to be scooped, not after all this.

The trip back was pretty much a carbon copy of my trip out, that is to say not much happened. I think I have a good title for the piece—"Positively Main Street"—but that's about all at this point. I have so much information to deal with, it's tough to know where to start. Or how... or for whom? I'd think every magazine in the *world* would want this stuff, but... guess I'll just have to see. I'll write some letters of inquiry, maybe.

Anything happen in the wake of my visit? Any calls from strange long-distance-type people? How about David Zimmerman, he sounded pretty shook up when I told him about our conversation? Bet he'll be in touch.

Don't worry about my writing anything Bob might not like. I wouldn't do that...not because I fear his wrath, necessarily—a wrath rumored terrible swift!—but because...well, just for old times' sake, too.

Will forward a sample of the story just as soon as it slips out the ends of my fingers. And please let me know anything...

Very best,
Toby

Telegram sent about November 1 to editorial staffs of the following magazines: *Esquire, Playboy, Harper's,* the *Atlantic Monthly,* the *Saturday Evening Post, Life,* and the *New Yorker.*

WORK IN PROGRESS. BOB DYLAN'S HIBBING, MINNESOTA. EX-CLUSIVE INTERVIEWS WITH FAMILY, TEACHERS, CHILDHOOD FRIENDS, AND "THE GIRL FROM THE NORTH COUNTRY." PLUS COLOR PHOTOS. IF INTERESTED PLEASE CONTACT TOBY THOMP-SON —— —— CABIN JOHN, MARYLAND, AS SOON AS POSSIBLE.

Response: Zero.

November 12, 1968

Dear Echo,

Haven't heard from you in a while, and it's been one of those days when the formal writing just won't come, so thought I'd drop the muse a line and see if she's still with me. Anything interesting going on?

Did you see Bob's picture on the cover of *The Saturday Evening Post?* Incredible! He sure seems different—no hair, baggy trousers, and what looks to my prep school eye like a Brooks Brothers shirt! Wonder why he consented to do that, have his picture on the cover of a big national mag. like the *Post?* And he's granted a *long* interview to *Sing Out!* magazine that's on the stands now...I wonder if he's planning to come out of seclusion? Hope I can get my story out before he does—or at least in step with his reappearance. He's due for a new album pretty soon, too. It's been about a year since *John Wesley Harding.*

I have a couple of questions about the letter-poem I wonder if you'd mind answering: (1) What is a hematite? (2) What was the paper he says he took from you when you first met? (3) What was the occasion of it being "20 below zero, and running down that road in the rain with yo' ol' man's flashlight on my ass. Now yo' mother shines it in my face."? (4) What about the time "when we sat and talked in the L & B 'til two o'clock at night," and "I was such a complete idiot, thinking back, that the car was in the driveway all night long."?

If you can remember the answers to any of the above, and could possibly drop me another line, I'd appreciate it very much. Hope all is well in the north country.

Very best,
Toby

P.S.: Enclosed is the sample I promised you a month ago.

T.

November 29, 1968

Dear Toby,

Got your letter the other day, so I guess I'd better hurry up and write, so you can continue.

No, David Zimmerman hasn't called me. I can't think of any reason why he really should. I don't think he'd have the nerve anyway. The last time I saw him he was very friendly and sweet and promised to take me to coffee sometime. I never saw him since.

Answer to question #1: A hematite is what Hibbing's name is for the class yearbook.

#2: The paper I think he's referring to was probably some of those limericks that get circulated around high schools every once in a while, or something. I'm not sure at all in fact, I'm only guessing. It could've been schoolwork or anything.

#3: My father didn't allow me to have boys over. That night my father and mother had left me babysitting my nephew. Bob and John came over. When my parents came home Bob and John jumped out the front door and ran down the road. My father heard them and was shining the flashlight on them as they were running down the road.°

#4: Bob's father must've grounded him and he wasn't supposed to use the car. I'm not sure but maybe his parents were out of town and he felt he should've just taken it.

I like your writing, although it makes me very achingly lonely for the past. I like where you say "our" man himself, because he does belong to all of us now. Those black loafers and bluejeans make me very lonesome, too. It's wonderful that you have such a good conception of how it actually was. It brings me right up there again.

Echo

Ah! The muse is pleased.

References and Random Wonderment

records: (1) *Music from Big Pink,* The Band. Three new or relatively new Dylan songs on this strange album. Straight from the mystic cornea of *John Wesley Harding.* Neighbors of Bob in Woodstock.

(2) *Sweetheart of the Rodeo,* The Byrds. Two more new Dylan tunes, with the same sort of reclusiveness expressed. But Bob seems to be giving his songs away fairly freely now. Signifying a break?

The following, a Christmas-card note from Echo:

December 26, 1968

Dear Toby,

I've been meaning to write. I guess this is as good a place as any. Sorry to do business at a time and place like this, but I'm afraid I must. I hope that you are not planning on trying to have what Bob wrote in my yearbook intact in your story. I wrote to the Sheltons, who know Bob very well and they called me last week and I didn't even tell them I sent you that copy, but I did tell them I had talked

---

° Just for fun, grab a listen to *Another Side of Bob Dylan*, side two, band one.

to you. They told me to be very careful as Bob is getting really peculiar and tried to sue some people who tried to have some old photographs published. Please believe me when I say that the Sheltons are both the nicest people and are only concerned about not upsetting Bob. He's very depressed lately. I suppose you've heard of the predictions of his committing suicide. It worries me. Anyway, it might be a good idea to not use what he wrote as it is; to get ideas to use from it is fine, but I'm just afraid he might be suing us both, if it was to be used exactly as written. I just couldn't afford that, and I couldn't stand for him to hate me either. Please let me know what you're doing. Just what kind of story is it, like for a magazine? Sixty pages doesn't sound like a book. Why do geniuses have to get funny! Write to me, maybe if I know what's going on I'll stop worrying. Okay? Thanks

HELLO!
MERRY CHRISTMAS TO YOU
AND A
HAPPY NEW YEAR!

and Good Luck!

Echo

January 14, 1969

Dear Echo,

For goodness sake calm down! I already told you I won't write anything bad, you don't have to worry about that. And as far as the letter-poem is concerned, I don't want to be sued either. I've quoted *one line* of the thing; he's not going to get upset about that little bit. I'm enclosing the last page of my manuscript so you can see I'm not fibbing.

Would like to write more, but am going nuts in the preparation of a typescript, so will sign off here. Think I'll try *Esquire* as a first market. Shoot for the stars, why not?

Best,
Toby

February 6, 1969, rejection received from *Esquire*. No comment, just a standard X-slip.

February 8, 1969, submitted typescript to the *Village Voice*. Will be surprised if they reject. Enough Dylan gossip in this thing to fill Howard Smith's "Scenes" column for a year.

Mid-February: No word from the *Voice* yet, but rumors have been flying concerning Bob's new album—a country collection—and the possibilities of a big concert tour. Bob's "comeback" could be at hand. If my story gets in print soon, and I don't get beaten out by Shelton's book, I should be in very good shape.

March 5: Howard Smith wrote in his column the other day that he's heard Bob's new album, that it is country music as predicted, and that a duet with Johnny Cash is included—of "Girl from the North Country," of all songs, Christ! And here's little Toby with the inside poop. What's the *Voice* waiting around for?

March 8: Couldn't stand it anymore, and called Daniel Wolfe, editor of the *Voice*. He put me on to Diane Fisher, an assistant editor and rock critic, and she apologized for the lack of a response, but she'd been out for a month . . . however, she wants the piece! to be run in conjunction with projected release date of Bob's new album, *Nashville Skyline*. Too perfect!

Friday, March 28, 1969 . . . San Francisco *Chronicle*

On the Town : : : : : : : : : : : :

A HOME-TOWN VIEW
OF BOB DYLAN
: : : : : : : : : : : Ralph J. Gleason

Determined students of the work and personality of Bob Dylan (Dylanologists of the world, Unite!) will be fascinated to read the new series of articles appearing in the *Village Voice*.

Beginning in the March 20 issue of the *Voice*, a young New York writer named Toby Thompson is publishing a series on Dylan beginning with a visit to his home town, Hibbing, Minnesota. It's about time somebody got around to that.

The *Voice* series looks like it is going to shatter the carefully built up story of Dylan's running away from home, his estrangement from his family and the rest. Thompson quotes a Hibbing resident as saying Dylan was in Hibbing for his father's funeral last spring.

"Just for a couple of days, but that didn't stop him from finding time to fix his mother up with a brand-new Cadillac and his brother David with a Buick. Those stories you read about Bob and his family... couldn't be farther from the truth ... Bob's a good family boy..."

It will be interesting to see if, in future articles in this series, Thompson casts any real light on the whole boyhood and early experiences of Dylan.

Telegram received from novelist William Crawford Woods, March 30, 1969:

ERNEST,
"BUT I KNOW WHAT YOU WANT." WELL DONE.
SCOTT.

April 14, 1969

Dear Toby,

You're so enthusiastic that I just have to take a few minutes off to drop you a note.

No, I haven't seen the article yet. Could you maybe wait until all the six parts have been published and then send me copies or photostats of the whole thing? I'd appreciate that very much. Or, we have a copy machine in the office, I could even copy it and send it back to you if you like.

I guess I goofed again, but that's the story of my life anyway. The Sheltons had wanted an exclusive interview, but I wrote to them and asked them to be more explicit, and they never answered. Well, it's too late now.

I'm so glad to hear about Bob's new album; and especially to hear that he's smiling. I saw the picture of him on the front of *Saturday Evening Post,* and he looks healthy even. I was so worried about all the predictions of the No. 1 Folk/Rock Singer supposed to commit suicide at Easter, and from what the Sheltons said about the way he was acting, I was afraid it would come to pass. Now Easter's over, and he's smiling and recording again. Spring is a good time of the year after all. I wonder if he ever really believed a long time ago that Johnny Cash would actually sing a duet with him.

Well, I'm doing this on company time, so I'd better cut it short. (That's one good excuse for my sloppy typing.)

Let me know any more good news.

Echo

CORRESPONDENCE/ASSORTED BUSINESS AND FAN

All received late April, early May.

E. S.
Flushing, N.Y.

Dear Mr. Thompson,

I had been assigned a term paper on Bob Dylan. Then I heard *The Village Voice* was featuring a continuing article on him. Because my report is due within 4 wks., and I don't know when the article will end, I was wondering if you'd be available for an interview to give me some additional information on Bob Dylan. If it is possible, would you please write me at the above address to inform me as to when it will be.

Thank you very much,
E. S.

M. A.
New York, N.Y.

Mr. Toby Thompson
THE VILLAGE VOICE
Sheridan Square
New York, N.Y. 10014

Dear Sir:

I have spent a great deal of time trying in the past year to obtain information about Bob Dylan, for a very good reason. I feel there is much depth to this young man. I have studied his records and spent much time trying to digest his thoughts. I was successful in securing after much carfare and wear and tear on my nerves a short picture book by a man named Kramer. Then I spent hours telephoning various places about Bob Dylan's book *Tarantula* which nobody ever heard of except persons I picked out to talk with in places like record shops, etc. I finally got through to the MacMillan publishers who informed me that the notice printed in the NY *Times* in March, 1969 was a mistake because the book had never been finished for publication. My next effort was in locating the book from the picture *Don't Look Back* which was too a terrible strain.

Only last week, I was told by somebody who knows of my interest in this subject that *The Village Voice* had run a series on Bob Dylan, but this person having no interest had discarded the copies.

This week I have spent in trying to track down this series and it took 4 days to make contact with *The Village Voice* since the lines were tied up or somebody would answer by saying "Hold on," go off and never come back. When I finally did get the *Voice* office I was told that the past issues were non-existent. Then I spent yesterday afternoon telephoning the libraries of the city hoping to round up back copies so that I could at least read them. Would you know that out of all the libraries I called only one had the issues in question. I spent two hours there last night reading the series and trying to figure a way to xerox the copies for myself. However the xerox machine at the library in question would not take the size of the paper. Today, I called the 43rd and 11th Avenue branch to find out, if by chance they might also have those back issues. No luck.

I would like to get the series and I will spend my own time typing a copy. This cannot be done at the public library, it would take days and be too disrupting to the public readers. Do you know how I can go about securing the series? I read it so quickly and making notes that I would like to have it. My mother is 71 years old. She is a Dylan fan and gulps up everything about him I bring home. But she does not go out. I would certainly like for her to enjoy the articles you wrote, although when I arrived home last night I tried to give her a short résumé of what I had read from the notes I took.

Thank you for whatever attention you can give this matter or any help you can offer. A reply will be appreciated. People just think one is truly mad in giving such energy to this type of interest.

Respectfully,
M. A.

SECOND TRIP

Just about a year ago
I set out on the road...
　　　　　—Creedence Clearwater
　　　　　　Revival, LODI*

* J. C. Fogerty-Jondora BMI

GUSHICON ONE: *A Poor Boy on the Street*

There's a lake behind the student union at the University of Wisconsin that laps a broad, concrete apron of the loveliest outdoor terrace in American academe. In early May the sailboats are out, and just before me in a carefully obstacled slew, two lion-maned students practiced maneuvering kayaks around and through clanging steel poles. I had driven from Chicago that morning—Oak Park, actually—and the sunshine, the metallic freshness of the lakeside air, and the kids in boats made it seem odd that I'd slept in such a town only hours before, that I was anywhere near Chicago and what it stood for this year, or that I was even in the United States. I could have been in Geneva, Garmisch-Partenkirchen, any of a hundred European lake-towns. But no: this was Madison, Wisconsin, plop in the middle of the American Midwest, and I was headed north again in search of Bobby Zimmerman... but with credentials this time. And on assignment.

Richard Goldstein had called; I picked up the phone one night about eleven thirty and it was he. Diane Fisher had given Goldstein my number, and he told me he simply had to have a follow-up story to my *Voice* piece for his new Bantam quarterly, *US*. I had been skeptical about a second trip, but he'd assured me he would pay my way back out—the possibility of a book was becoming more attractive, and I would have to make a second trip anyway for extra photos—so I considered the whole thing an honor. I'd been a fan of Goldstein's, but I'd never agreed with what he wrote about

Dylan. My little fantasies about Bob and his music were as stub-
bornly personal as the next fellow's.

I'd always wanted to publish something about Dylan . . . at least
since my sophomore year in college when I got an A on a paper
about his songs and poetry in the first graduate-level English course
I ever took. It was taught by the poet Robert Huff—a wildman—
and he'd read my paper in class. That was 1964. Huff's handwritten
comment had been classically foreboding: "Beware of a too wildly
journalistic style for this kind of writing." Dylan had been good to
me over the years . . . and his songs were of course a staple of my
repertoire. He'd gotten me girls, grades, money for performing,
money for writing, and a head start in the New Journalism. I felt a
certain obligation to continue our relationship.

Here I was back on the road, headed to Hibbing. And Minneapolis, yes. A letter from Zachary Baker in my jeans, I was to call
his sister tonight. She used to date Dylan. Would that pan out? If
not, I had Echo! Was to meet her tomorrow afternoon in Minneapolis, to drive on up to Hibbing for a weekend picture-taking
session. "The Girl from the North Country" for a weekend in Bob
Dylan's hometown!—the spots she could show me. The pictures
I'd have!

Things were quiet in Madison. The University of Wisconsin, scene
of the worst campus rioting in the Midwest, hadn't copped any
Huntley/Brinkley airtime in months. Everyone looked wild-eyed
and radical as could be, but there wasn't any action. Too bad—
I could cover it if there were. Wisconsin was a great campus to
visit. I had a friend, P., in the English Department whom I'd run
into the last time I was out and he'd shown me around, stoned me,
and put me up. I hoped he would do the same this evening. But
Wisconsin's student union! Last time I had been out, the Electric
Circus light show and traveling band had performed there, and
the whole frigging school it seemed showed up, all spaced, lighting
up right there in the auditorium, and nobody was busted, nobody
hassled. Rumor has it that there is more narcotics traffic in Madison, Wisconsin, than in the entire rest of the Midwest. I half be-

lieve it. The beautiful old beer hall in the basement of the student union sells hardly a beer a day, now. Everybody's zonked on Cokes.

The Revolution and Madison, and black students' rights and rent control and me, back on the Bobby Zimmerman story. Did it fit? I'd picked up a girl hitchhiking on the way into Madison, a student, and naturally I'd told her what I was doing out here with East Coast plates and a VW full of typewriters and briefcases and old *Village Voices*, and she hadn't blinked. She said a few negative things about *Nashville Skyline*, but that was it. I drank a cup of coffee with her in the student union, and the last thing she asked before leaving for her Revolution in Latin America class was, "How about it . . . level with me. Just where *is* Dylan's head with this apolitical stuff, anyway? And singing with Johnny Cash, he supported Nixon, didn't he? Is Dylan dropping out on us?"

I couldn't answer; I mumbled something and she left abruptly. What *was* Bob doing with his new countrified album? I hadn't found it startling at first, because Bob had always been essentially either a blues or a country musician, heavily influenced by the raunchiest of roots. But people didn't remember that; they remembered his "Mr. Tambourine Man" and "Like a Rolling Stone" sounds, not the bluegrass, "Blowin' in the Wind" supertwang. What I'd found fascinating about *Nashville Skyline* was (1) that every song was pure love, not hate-love or muse-love or love-for-irony's-sake as most of his songs had been in the past, but good old moon-in June, will-you-still-love-me-tomorrow? schlock, (2) his persistent and masterful use of clichés—practically every other word and phrase on the album is a well-wrought cliché, seemingly for cliché's sake, but without the usual offense, (3) that he should choose "Girl from the North Country" to kick off the album, one of two "love" songs he'd recorded previously—the other being "One Too Many Mornings," likewise a lament for Minnesota, (4) and that his much-made-of pose on *Nashville Skyline*'s cover was a perfect mimicry of Ric von Schmidt's hat-tipping salutation on a record cover clearly visible in the color photo of Bob on *Bringin' It All Back Home*—on Bob's first album, he had paid tribute to von

Schmidt with the classic "Baby Let Me Follow You Down." All this seemed to add up to what the Beatles were singing these days, "Get back, get back, get back to where you once belonged." But it was impossible to tell for sure; I could get back out to Hibbing and have another look-see, though.

The Midwest had changed since the previous fall. The whole country had, of course, but here in the heartland of America with all of Richard Nixon's forgotten Americans right there on street corners, factions were polarized. Wisconsin, the whole *state,* was practically a battlefield. There were the long-hairs, and then there were the honest-to-God-fearing citizens. Gas station attendants refused to wait on you if you wore blue jeans and weren't a farmer. Old ladies scowled. Shopkeepers were careful to let on that they despised serving you. The situation was intolerable; there were too many aliens in sleepy hollow.

And Chicago: last evening, round about Toledo, I'd promised myself that I was going to spend the night in Oak Park, Illinois—Hemingway's hometown. I had Carlos Baker's biography tucked into my valise, and it shouldn't have been too hard to find Hemingway's old house. But naturally, I'd gotten lost. There are only two stayable hotels in Oak Park, and they're blocks apart . . . Chicago, *the border,* is very close though. I'd strayed across, and drove around for half an hour trying to find my way out—until I spied a friendly police car. Sure, I stopped and asked directions . . . thirteen hours on the road had dulled my senses. I realized my mistake real quick, however, once I pulled alongside the cruiser and got a look at those two, blue-helmeted faces. They responded to my plea for directions by shining a spotlight in my eyes and telling me I'd better get my ass off the street before they locked it up.

And Oak Park was no consolation. No wonder Hemingway was so mad! *Hibbing* is more up-to-date and sophisticated—you can't get a drink in Oak Park . . . Ernest Hemingway's hometown, a dry burg! The desk clerk at the Oak Hotel had heard of Papa, but she didn't know where his house was. In *Hibbing* desk clerks knew where Bob's house was. I had to go way across the Eisenhower Expressway to get a beer, probably just like Hemingway had had to, in the old days before there was even an *Eisenhower.*

His old house at 600 North Kenilworth Avenue—the one he wrote about in "Soldier's Home" and other Nick Adams–type stories—it's still there, still painted gray with a big fireplace in the living room that somebody else sits in now. Somebody else's tricycles are in the front yard, and there isn't any Historical Society plaque on the door or marker in the street. I stood around outside for a long time; nobody was home. Then I sat on Papa's front step and thought about his grave in Ketchum, Idaho. And his boyhood in Oak Park. And how one couldn't have happened without the other.

The afternoon was growing cold, and waves on the lake were kicking up miniature whitecaps over the bows of the kayaks. But the two lion-manes didn't care; there was enough sun to go around, and the exercise was good. A tall girl with waist-length hair, pitch black against a heavy Irish sweater—off-white with heavy ribbing—whisked past me and on down to the edge of the lake. She waved enthusiastically to the kayaks, and sat down to pull off her high leather boots. She had a pair of Topsiders in her bookbag. One of the lion-manes paddled over and docked. He kissed her on the top of the head and walked over to a shed. The girl was laughing, trying to tie her Topsiders with half a lifejacket on. She could hardly reach. The lion-mane dragged another kayak out of the shed and slipped it into the water for the girl. She had her own paddle. The water was rough by the edge of the dock, but she got in without shipping any water, and cinched the rubber skirt up around her waist . . . it fit under her bust like an Empire gown. Lion-mane shoved off behind her and they took a turn around the obstacle course together. The girl was good; she didn't clang a pole the first time through, but on the second try she almost capsized in a big wave. She was still smiling; her hair hung down below the skirt at her waist and trailed in the water. I thought about her smile and what she might have been like in Oak Park, Illinois, or at Sammy's Pizza Palace in Hibbing. I bet *she* liked *Nashville Skyline,* and I bet she'd like to read about the 1957 Jacket Jamboree Talent Festival, or maybe even sit on Ernest Hemingway's old lawn. Or Bob Dylan's bed. I watched her go through the course once more, but then my friend P. was coming across the terrace, smiling, and he looked like he was stoned. We shook hands and waved at the kayaks, and the girl pointed with her paddle and laughed.

CONFUSICON: *Madison, 2, 3, and 4*

Pieces of pink paper on my tongue stuck sweet as the phone rang at Ellen Baker's in Minneapolis a long ways off, and one of P.'s fellow professors ran a shower down the hall the water was rushing and P. couldn't stop giggling I hoped I wouldn't, his black faculty club dresser and Victorian wardrobe depressing in the corner, was he a sad fellow to stay here with old men wrapped in New York *Times?* he spoke still young and wore his towel to the shower room, didn't carry it over his shoulder a light-blue bathrobe in defeat like the others Mr. Chips not he, the smoke was talking and a voice drifted into the receiver, Ellen Baker, hi, you see your brother wrote me this letter and I don't mean to bother but . . . oh yes, he wrote you he wrote me, and you would? that's fine tomorrow I'll be in Minneapolis, no I'm sorry excuse me that's my friend and he's watching television, yes, I'm laughing too it's very funny stuff, please pardon, oh I know, yes, because you're so fond of your brother he's so cute, oh he is? his letter was charming . . . your mother too, she knew Bob knew him well, could she come tomorrow I'd appreciate meeting her any and every little bit, you'll have to excuse me *please P. turn off the television,* I'm sorry oh god I guess I'd better wait until tomorrow to talk further, you're very kind with a nice sense of humor I can tell, fine, will call tomorrow as soon as I hit town, hee hee, oh god

WHY, said the first stoned Hippy friend of P.'s, ARE YOU DOING THIS TO DYLAN, I READ YOUR *VOICE* SERIES AND

TELL ME ONE THING, *WHY* ARE YOU VIOLATING HIS PAST, WILL IT DO ANYBODY ANY GOOD, I'D JUST LIKE TO KNOW, YOU DON'T SEEM TO BE THE KIND OF GUY WHO'D WANT TO HURT ANYBODY, *WHY?*

WHO, said the second stoned Hippy friend of P.'s, mustachioed one who rolled joints fat as Marsh Wheelings and who wouldn't stop, wouldn't stop, *WHO* DO YOU THINK YOU ARE DIGGING AROUND IN BUSINESS THAT'S NOBODY'S BUT BOB'S, *WHO* DO YOU THINK WILL CONDONE IT, DYLAN FANS? THEY KNOW THE ONE AREA BOB HAS ALWAYS ASKED THEM NOT TO EXPLORE, HIS PAST! DOCUMENT THE REVOLUTION, THE NOW, NOT THE THEN!

WHAT, said the third stoned Hippy friend of P.'s, ARE WE TO GAIN FROM THIS? WILL OUR PEOPLE LEARN ABOUT THEMSELVES FROM YOUR WRITING, WILL THEY SEE HOW A GREAT ONE HAS RISEN FROM CRUMBY BEGINNINGS TO THE POSITION OF MOST EXALTED, WILL THEY TAKE HEED AND FOLLOW? WHAT GOOD WILL FLOW IN THE WAKE OF YOUR FINDINGS?

gosh,

i was just trying to write a little story about Bob in hibbing as a kid and what it was like then, i didn't mean anybody any harm certainly not him i hope he doesn't take offense, i've always been aware of what he told journalists about his privacy but after all he's authorized a biography and given names to robert shelton for him to seek these people out, some of the same people i talked to and shelton's an old man what does he know about growing up in the fifties and wanting to be a rock and roll star? you know what kind of a book he's going to write, although i'm sure it'll be good in its way, but we need a kid's eye view, like mine or yours but i just happened to be there like bob always says there is no eye and he can't even speak the word eye anymore i wish i didn't feel guilty but i do and you assholes aren't making me feel any better, P. let's split it's past time for me to go, Minneapolis and all those old girlfriends await, feel like i'm going home, maybe that's it i identify too closely, but i wouldn't want to *be* bob, how could i, i suppose i already am, that's the justification and the need! we *all* are, doesn't that make it better now

At seven thirty in the morning, engineers and a handful of Arts and Science students are the only people sipping coffee in Wisconsin's student union cafeteria. They huddle bleary-eyed and half-conscious over their styrofoam cups, heads swallowed by textbooks or bent around charts. Kitchen help sweeps up; you constantly have to rearrange your feet. You drink your coffee, exchange addresses and telephone numbers with your friend, and get up to leave. Nobody notices you. We are asleep in America.

Out front of the student union you unlock your car, flick the parking ticket you will never pay off your windshield, and root around in your backseat for your Powr-House Blue Denim Engineer's cap. On the way out of town, a service station manager is comfortably surly... but he tells you how to find your way back to the highway. Even he can sympathize with that need. Outside the state capitol, six or seven antiwar protestors with black coffins and signs are getting an early start. You wonder if their number will increase as this spring morning lengthens. It is a possibility; the demonstrators' faces are set in defiance as they march around State Circle, and they are oblivious to catcalls from the rush-hour traffic. One of their signs reads "Come senators, congressmen please heed the call/Don't block up the doorway, don't stand in the hall." Bob's songs still covered a lot of ground, if he didn't. Comforting. But you are eight hundred miles away and ten years behind before you hear the news—"Madison, Wisconsin has erupted in the worst campus rioting of the spring." Huntley/Brinkley Report. You might have covered it; yes, but hopefully you'll have a better perspective from where you are.

GUSHICON TWO: *Gophers*

Minnesota, once again. Bob's beginning, and in a very real sense, mine. "The land of sky-blue water," "vacation land," and Minneapolis, "city on the water"—from a combination of the American Indian and Greek. Minneapolis/St. Paul, "the twin cities," how homey... *big* industrial town, home of the largest linseed oil mills in the world saith the *Encyclopedia Britannica,* with magno flour production, many foundries, machine and railroad shops, factories that make artificial limbs, factories that make hearing aids... *good* baseball team, *good* football team, lots of money, the Mississippi River running right down to the Gulf of Mexico—an outlet to the sea!— the Mississippi, bisector of the country, now you're East, now you're West, traditional folk getaway and natural balm, *you haven't lived unless you've tried it,* innocence-and-experience, good-and-evil, McCarthy-and-Humphrey, F. Scott Fitzgerald's hometown... though his ancestors were from Maryland, and he is buried ten miles from where I live in that state... lots of other famous people; but the East and the West! the River, these are the things that make Minneapolis/St. Paul an important American symbol. Home of Echo, the "Girl from the North Country," home of the University of Minnesota, Bob's first excuse for escape, scene of Bob's first "professional" performances, place where I was to meet Ellen Baker.

Slip into huge, concrete shopping center on the St. Paul side of town, purchase pint of Cutty Sark just in case gosh knows what'd happen, slap it in the glove compartment, and find a phone booth where I can call Ellen. She's there right where she promised she'd be, at UNIVAC work, and she'll meet me in half an hour at her house . . . gives me directions, and I set out. Across construction, over huge new superhighways being laid into the land, through a semi-dingy part of town, to Ellen's neighborhood—quaint, quiet, and vaguely faculty-ish.

There it was, her house, but I was early and felt strange. All this was somehow different from last time out. I sensed excitement and a little fear in my gut at the prospect of meeting another of Bob's old friends, but . . . it seemed, well, *professional.* The freedom of my last excursion was missing—I knew I didn't have to write this story if things didn't pan out. Goldstein had assured me he would handle trip expenses whether I filed a story or not—and I found myself checking my pockets for pencils and notebooks, worrying whether I would be able to remember what Ellen said, and looking at my watch. Spring was different, too. The urgency of autumn was lacking, that desperation . . . I hoped I got lots of money for my book.

Ellen's house was an apartment building in disguise, a former house, granted, but presently sliced up into various ways-to-live. Her door was very brown, and the hallway *smelled* brown. She answered her bell at the first knock, and *she* was brown . . . not her skin, that was very white, but her hair, and her shoes, and the way she shook my hand.

"Hi," she said. "You *are* young."

"Had you expected someone fat and gray?"

"No"—she laughed—"but a friend was telling me about your *Voice* story, and said you sounded young. I hope I didn't offend you," smiling. She swept me into the living room—attractively arty: bookshelves lining the walls and supporting various expressionistic knickknacks, ashtrays of noble design, a poster-papered yellow basket with real dollar bills stuck in—and plopped me down on a couch. "Can I get you something—coffee, a beer?"

"Beer's fine, thanks."

Ellen disappeared for a moment into a pinup decorated kitchen at the far end of the apartment; her voice, loud but not harsh, carrying clearly from the other room, over icebox sounds and running water. She apologized for the fact that her mother couldn't make it, but felt she could tell me anything I might want to know, without her parent's assistance. Besides, Ellen's mother hadn't wanted to get involved. And the only reason Ellen was seeing me was for her little brother Zachary. He had been so excited.

"'Robert, you have green teeth' my mother used to say, and she would tell him either to go brush his teeth and take a shower, or not come to the dinner table. My mother was the only person I ever knew who could make Bob mind; and the only one who could talk to him like that and not make him mad. Bob was an extremely headstrong young man." Ellen emerged from the kitchen, batik skirt swishing and closely cropped brown hair electrically askew, with a Löwenbrau for me and a cocktail for herself. She settled on the coffee table directly in front of the couch where I was sitting, crossed her legs primly, and continued. I pulled out my pencil and notebook.

"I met Bob the first part of our freshman year together here at the University of Minnesota—at a friend's house, fellow named David Whittaker. Bob was sitting over in the corner, with his guitar I think, looking so cute and helpless I immediately liked him. David introduced him to me as 'Bob Dylan' too. He was using that name exclusively by then. He didn't tell me his real name until much later, when we'd become very good friends. Bob didn't like 'Zimmerman' at all. He used to tell us 'Dylan' was his mother's maiden name and that he preferred it to his father's. Of course, that wasn't true either, but we didn't care. Bob had quite an imagination."

"Could you spell 'Whittaker,' please?"

She did.

"Bob used to introduce himself to people by all sorts of different names. He was such a role-player. I even heard him say at a strange party once that he was Bobby Vee, you know, that old rock and roll crooner-type. People were saying 'Hey, that's Bobby Vee!' and pointing and whispering all evening. Bob just smiled and made up success stories, never letting on that he wasn't really Bobby Vee. We laughed about it later, but Bob was spooky about those things. I think he actually believed himself sometimes." Ellen laughed.

"How did your mother get involved with Bob?" I was intrigued by that. "Zachary said in his letter that Bob played for one of your mother's classes."

"Yes, for my mother's fifth-grade class at Horace Mann school, right here in town. He did a few songs with a good friend of ours, a boy named Fred Hoffman. Fred played the guitar, too. But that was a long time after Bob started hanging around our house. My mother became very fond of Bob, after she saw that his interest in me was aboveboard, and that his grooming and dress didn't reflect some subterranean sloppiness. She was always a sucker for strays. I suppose Bob dined and slept at our house on a fairly regular basis for over four months. He hardly ever seemed to have a place to live. But he liked our house just fine . . . besides having both my mother and me charmed and a free place to stay, he had my father's huge collection of bound folk music to peruse."

"What kind of stuff was in that?"

"Well, my father was quite a collector. He had old manuscripts, sheet music, and folk magazines. Bob and I would sit for hours digging through those. Father had some old records, too. Old 78s. We'd listen to those all the time—songs like 'Those Brown Eyes' by Cisco Houston and Woody Guthrie, and 'Go Down You Murderers.' Bob would sing that one every time he'd have too much to drink, over and over." Ellen paused, staring off into a cluttered, bookshelved corner. I followed her eyes, and the space on the floor there looked very empty.

"We'd sing those old songs together sometimes, too. Just for fun. I never performed with Bob, but we'd harmonize old tunes from my father's records, and songs that were the type Bob was doing then. Not the bluesy stuff he picked up later, but traditional things, sort of A-minorish folky."

"I don't suppose he was doing any rock?"

"Heavens no, that was out of fashion. *Nobody* in the folk set played rock and roll. They all did the same sort of stuff as Bob— traditional ballads. Nobody seemed to be writing any songs, either. Bob was fairly competent on the guitar, and would do his own fledgling arrangements, but I don't think he was composing. He was too unsure of himself then."

"How so?" Didn't sound like the Hibbing Bob I knew.

"Well...Bob was extremely inarticulate unless either he had a guitar in his hands and was making love to you by singing, had some sort of hat on his head, any kind, or was drunk. Then he'd sit there on the floor with his feet curled up underneath him, and be absolutely magnificent. Strangers at parties would ask 'Who's that?' and people wouldn't let him stop. He'd just sit there playing and grinning...with those Hush Puppies on."

"Bob wore *Hush Puppies?*"

"Sure. He pledged a fraternity, too, did you know that?"

"I'd heard he *lived* at one, but...."

"Sigma Alpha Mu, the Jewish house."

"Bob Dylan was a Sammy?"

"That's right." Ellen laughed. "Bob was a pledge. But he left fairly early in the year. *That* really wasn't his scene, even then. Bob was serious about his schoolwork for a while, too. At the very start. He tried hard, but it wasn't him. He finally decided he just wanted to play the guitar and party. He drank an awful lot in those days— and as I said, he could reach a point in his drunk where he would become brilliantly articulate; but if he slipped past that point, he'd become sloppy and unintelligible. I don't think Bob looked at a book after the first month he was at the university. College wasn't the reason he hung around. Minneapolis, as backward as it might seem to you, was nevertheless the first big town Bob ever lived in. He'd never admit to a stranger that he came from Hibbing."

There was suddenly the click of a key in the front door lock, and Ellen's husband walked in. I was introduced to a youngish, vaguely smiling fellow who was *also* brown, and we shook hands. He disappeared almost immediately into a room at the rear of the apartment. I poured myself another glass of beer and tried to think of something to ask.

"What about other old friends of Bob's who might still be around Minneapolis? Are there any left?"

"Not to speak of, really. I ran into the fellow who used to run the Scholar. He was working in a parking lot. But I wouldn't bother with him, he's not so easy to talk to. A girl Bob was considering getting married to at one point—I think she's still in town, but I don't know where, or what her married name is now. All those people were strange—friends in a weird way. 'That Itinerant Jewish Folksinger' is what some of them used to call Bob. Not everyone was quite so taken with his unique variety of charm as my family and I. We were probably a little more eccentric than most of the people around Minneapolis, liked music more, and enjoyed taking care of attractive no-accounts. Bob had quite a few good friends, don't get me wrong, but he was extremely hard to get to know well. Part of it was his just being inarticulate, but there was also a very definite streak of cynicism in Bob. He could be warm on the surface, but that tough attitude a little way down always seemed to show through. The Jewish business was a good bit of it. Minnesota— and Minneapolis in particular—for a long while was the seat of anti-Semitism for practically the entire country.

"And Bob wanted so much to be one of the people he sang about. I used to kid him by saying, 'How's the man of the soil, to-day?' He wanted to be a 'man of the soil' more than anything else. But how could you be a man of the soil and be Jewish? Especially with a name like 'Zimmerman.'"

The pages were coming unglued from my notebook, I was writing so fast. This was stuff Echo *never* could have provided me with: small-time Bob, on his own in the big city.

"Those stories about Bob idolizing Woody Guthrie are true, too. Bob talked about going East to meet Woody all the time. He'd say, 'We're gonna go see him, Ellen, pretty soon!' We'd sing Woody's songs all afternoon, play my father's old records . . . and I think it was just about that time that Bob got a harmonica. We'd be at a party or someplace, and Bob would have been drinking to just past that point, and somebody would say, 'Woody's outside, Bob. Woody wants to meet you.' Bob's head would jerk up, and sometimes he'd stumble outside screaming, 'I'm coming, Woody, I'm coming!'"

"Jesus."

Ellen twirls the ice in her glass, and nods. "Exactly. I never thought that was a nice trick to play, but some of our other friends did, and wouldn't have missed it for the world."

I jotted a few notes in silence. Ellen was quiet, so I continued, backtracking and rephrasing various things I'd scribbled.

"Think you could show me some of the places where you and Bob used to hang out? Dinkytown and all that? If you have time, I mean."

"I suppose so—though there isn't too much of anything left. Sure . . . if *I* can drive." Ellen put down her glass and stood up.

"By all means."

"Let me tell my husband."

GUSHICON THREE: *On the Side That's Winning*

Ellen Baker wheeled her ancient Citroën through turns and away from stoplights with tough expertise; Ellen Baker was impressive. I tried to load my camera in the lurch and sway of the big car's foam-cushioned seats, and could not. I wanted a picture of this person behind the wheel. She downshifted to a stop sign and I pleaded for time to load.

"It's not hard to see why you wanted to drive."

"Yes, well, I used to be a professional stock car driver. Nothing international or superglamorous, just races around the state." The car idled uneasily as I stuffed a roll of Tri-X into my camera.

"Powder-puff derby affairs?"

"Nope, the real thing. No sex discrimination where the big money is, at least not in these parts. I didn't do too badly, either."

"I shouldn't think you would have." We roared away from the stop sign and continued down a broad avenue, past a sports arena and practice field where the university holds its games and pro teams occasionally work out, on past classroom-type buildings and fraternity houses, to a honking, scrambling intersection.

"This," Ellen exclaimed, "is Fourth Street." She pulled to the curb for a moment and put the car in neutral.

"Whether or not this Fourth Street is 'positively' the one, who can say but Bob? Everyone here in Dinkytown thought their main drag was the one Bob sings about, though. It makes sense. Dinkytown is the student neighborhood where not just Bob lived, but everyone he hung around with. The Scholar and Bastille coffee houses were in Dinkytown. And as you can see, now that we're on it, Fourth Street would represent all of that to Bob, the social scene, the university crud . . . the old folk people."

"Let's park and walk around."

"OK, but it's pretty hard to find a place." Ellen pulled the Citroën away from the curb and crossed the street. She swung into a lot behind a variety shop, and cut the engine. But an attendant walked over as we were getting out and told her she had to move her car. Ellen argued, but the fellow had her dead to rights. So she switched out of that particular variety-store space to one of several reserved for customers of a hardware store. She locked up the Citroën, and we laughed our way out of the lot.

"We'll have to go into the hardware store and browse though"— Ellen frowned mockingly—"so we won't have any broken any rules."

Fourth Street welcomed us with hot, gray breath . . . a summer greeting reminiscent of New York in July, not what one would have expected of Minnesota in May. We strolled past student-quarter tobacco and leather shops, hole-in-the-wall diners, a Baskins and Robbins ice cream parlor, Gray's drugstore—where Ellen said she and Bob used to sip sodas, the College Hotel . . . and a brand-new Burger King, on the site of the old Ten O'Clock Scholar. I was snapping pictures all over the place, posing Ellen, trying to get as much of Fourth Street as I could into each shot, thinking about light, thinking about what spots might have been early Bobby Dielan-type hangouts, asking Ellen . . .

She stopped in front of our hardware store, at a small, outdoor potpourri of jangling metal things, and picked up a little silver bucket. "Look"—she whistled—"it's galvanized, just like a shiny new garbage can! Can't pass that up." She paid the man, checked herself in the pail's mirrorlike surface, and we walked on down the block. "*This* is our ticket out of the parking lot." Kids were hustling up the street, old men were huddled around another sidewalk display in front of a movie theater—this one of old clothes—there was music playing from a record store near a busy railroad overpass, people were buying Burger King burgers by the bagful, ice cream cones in the amusement-park heat . . . no sadness, no Hibbing regrets . . . just cars and noise and life, and no real thoughts of Bob.

"What about drugs? Were there many around when he was here? Did he have any connection with that sort of thing?"

"Sure. There were drugs around; there have always been drugs around. But Bob never indulged. Not when I knew him, anyway. Drugs were associated with hoods in black leather jackets who rode motorcycles and listened to rock and roll. The folk set wouldn't have had anything to do with that. It just wasn't 'Dinkytown.'" Ellen and I stopped at the corner of Fourth Street and Sixteenth Avenue, and waited for the light to change. "I can remember Bob seeing somebody he didn't know—a girl usually, at a party or someplace— and hearing him say things like 'Never saw *her* around Dinkytown before.' That was the criterion. Had to be from Dinkytown."

We made our way back to Ellen's car, slipped in, and swung out of the lot toward center city. We drove along in silence, past fraternity houses alive with touch football and T-shirted inmates washing windows or sweeping steps, down tree-canopied lanes, professorial in their bricked silence—finally pulling to the side of the road in front of a shabby complex of light-green houses.

"What's this?" I inquired rather abruptly. Ellen turned toward me slowly, with a perturbed arch of her eyebrows. "Right there . . . 711 Fifteenth Street, that middle row house . . . that's where Bob lived for a few months with a couple of his friends—Hugh Brown and a terrible boy named Dirty Max."

"What was it like?"

"Absolutely horrible. I wouldn't even go over there unless I had to, and then I'd make certain to stay downstairs."

"That bad?"

"You couldn't imagine. But one day I was waiting there for Bob, to go someplace or do something, I don't know . . . Bob was getting dressed . . . when Dirty Max screamed down from the bathroom, 'Hey Ellen, come scrub my back.' Well, it wasn't every day a girl got to scrub a back like Dirty Max's, so I went on up. What an experience! Bob and I howled."

I was putting another roll of film in my camera and checking my light meter. "Is Dirty Max still in town?"

"Nope. Neither is Hugh Brown. I guess there really aren't too many of us left."

Across the street in front of Bob's old residence were half a dozen tennis courts, potholed and sagging. Several first-generation ladies jabbered their way down the block. A kid with a wagon stopped next door to 711, and called the name of a pal. I snapped several pictures and rejoined Ellen in the car. She had been sitting, waiting behind the wheel, staring straight ahead.

"Get what you wanted?"

"I suppose so. But hey, how about spinning down by the campus?"

"OK. I can show you where the old Sigma Alpha Mu house is, too." Ellen pulled out into the street, and I turned back toward 711 Fifteenth Street for one last look. Why hadn't I bothered to go inside? "But don't get your hopes up, I'm not even certain it's still there."

"Oh. No, that's all right."

We cut past a series of grassy lawns in front of university buildings, and Ellen pointed out one where she and Bob used to sunbathe in Minnesota's late-spring relief from winter. "Bob and I would spread out on the grass here on those rare, warm afternoons and watch people go by. Bob loved doing that, just watching people, imagining things. Especially about girls. Those first warm days after a Minnesota winter drive *everyone* crazy out here, but Bob seemed to react even more insanely than most. He'd positively melt. He'd lie on his stomach with his blue eyes twice their normal size, until I'd have to nudge him to remind him we had to go to class. Then he'd shake his head and smile in that cute way, and say, 'You go ahead Ellen, I'll meet you. I can't get up right now.' Usually I'd leave him lying there on his stomach, laughing and still staring."

"You make him sound like quite a lover."

Ellen laughed and threw the Citroën up in third gear. "Bob was funny about his women. At first he seemed very shy, sort of scared . . . but it didn't take long before you found out a good deal of that was an act. Bob was *surprisingly* amorous, and undiscriminating! He'd see a girl on the street or at a party, and it didn't matter what she looked like or who she was with, if he was in that mood."

"Thank God for the old frontier spirit."

"But Bob and I just weren't that way. Gradually, he started coming over to dinner less and less, and we'd run into each other by accident on the street, say hello...later, when we'd stopped seeing one another altogether and I'd heard he'd actually gone East, I was surprised. But not worried. I knew that little-boy helplessness of his that made him so attractive to women here in Minnesota wouldn't let him down in New York. He'd survive."

Ellen was cruising slowly through the twisting driveways of the university, shady and archetypically collegiate in their half hustle, half repose. Students were draped across the lawns or slouched against trees in poses of disconcern. A few labored under huge bundles of books, swaying toward that eternal carrel in the bowels of some anonymous building. It was difficult to picture Bob as part of such a setting.

"Have you seen him since he left college?" I asked. "Since he's really gotten big?"

"Uh-huh, twice...both times here in Minneapolis. The first was down by the river, a couple of years after he'd gone East. Joan Baez was in town for a concert at the university, and I had no idea Bob was back. But my husband and I were strolling along that afternoon, and here come Bob and Joan Baez on bicycles. The situation was doubly shocking, you see, because my husband used to know Joan Baez back in Cambridge. We all stopped and said hello, but Bob was sort of abrupt. The other time, Bob was here for a concert and a bunch of us from the old crowd went backstage. He didn't have much to say that night either."

Ellen stopped the big Citroën in the middle of a block, and looked around. "Well, just as I thought. The old fraternity house is gone, too."

"How long was it before you heard Bob was making it in New York?" I interrupted, not wanting her to lose track.

"That was funny, not long at all. I was in Cambridge visiting my husband—oh, about a year and a half after Bob left Minnesota—and I was in some club that was so small it didn't even have a john. You had to go upstairs through a record store. Anyhow, I was on my way to the john through this shop when I spied Bob's record. It was taped up in the window, staring right at me. That same pudgy face. I can remember stopping and saying to myself, 'Well! You actually *did* make it!'"

GUSHICON FOUR: *Sis-Boom-Boola, Were You There? Were You There?*

Ellen Baker had dropped me at my car, and we had said good-bye in front of her house; but now all that was history, and I was standing across the street from the new chapter house of Sigma Alpha Mu. It was just an ordinary house—not Georgian brick, or anything special—except for its green-shingled roof with Greek letters of the fraternity embossed in white. It looked vaguely like a utility hangar at a large rural airport. But not unattractive. I stepped over a fellow lounging in the grass, and angled up a good shot. I was almost out of film.

"That's a pretty nice roof, isn't it?" the fellow said.

"Excuse me?"

"I said that's a pretty nice roof. I put it on myself. I'm happy to see you like it well enough to take a picture." The fellow stood up and offered his hand. "My name's Barry. What are you, a reporter or something?"

I unfolded the saga once again. Barry listened politely, if at first a trifle confused as to all the fuss, and consented to show me around the fraternity. He was president, of course; I never seemed to run into anyone but the most important members of anything.

"We can look in the old scrapbooks, 1959 and '60, but I don't think we'll find much. There are plenty of pictures of the old house, but none I've ever seen of Dylan. I can remember fellows talking about him, the older guys ... but gosh, that was way back when *I* was pledging. Apparently he wasn't here very long—left after a couple of months, quit his pledging. Wanted to be alone with his music, I guess. We've had other folksingers here, too, and none of them seem to like fraternity life a whole lot..."

Several of the brothers had gathered around, popping the tops off sixteen-ounce cans of Schlitz, getting primed for the weekend—Friday afternoon at the house!—and cautiously checking me out. "Tell him to call Lenny Levine," a voice bellowed from upstairs. "He pledged the same year as Dylan. He'd know all about him."

Barry gave me a half-disgusted shake of his head, and continued to leaf through three huge scrapbooks. There were hundreds of pictures... Polynesian weekends, homecoming floats, the old house flooded for a party, with a waterfall roaring down the stairs into a pond full of live turtles and fish... but not even a pledge-class shot of Bob.

"Tell him to call Lenny Levine, why doncha?"

Barry snapped the last of the scrapbooks shut, and apologized for not being more help. One of the other guys suggested his older brother, Ted Litman, as a possible lead. Ted had been around. I took down his number, but was pretty sure I couldn't call. Somebody else mentioned the fact that Bob's Goldfine cousins from Hibbing lived at the sorority house just around the block. But... my mind was on Echo. I was supposed to call her before she left work, and it was almost five.

"Mind if I use your phone? I have an important call to make." Barry pointed over his shoulder to a rather damaged-looking corner of the room. "Of course not, but it'll cost you a dime just like the rest of us. Pay job." The phone-booth corner was classic—numbers scrawled everywhere, mild obscenities, ashes on the wall from stubbed-out cigarettes, the stench of overlong conversations. Took me back. I'd pledged a little time in phone booths like this, and, yes, had even joined a fraternity—but I'd dropped out of my pledge class, too. Sigma Phi Epsilon, 1963, "Sig Ep." Echo's office phone was ringing.

"Well, hi!" She laughed. "I thought you'd missed the boat."

"I told you I'd call before you left work, didn't I?"

"Yes, but you always cut it so close!"

We made arrangements to meet at her place, talked for a few moments longer, and signed off in fine form. I grinned my way back to Barry and the boys with hope in my heart. "Who's got a beer?" But something clicked, and I noticed, for the first time, an ancient piano crowded into one corner of Sigma Alpha Mu's sunporch. "Was that piano at the old house?"

"Sure was"—Barry blinked—"I never even thought about *that* before." Wow, nothing could go wrong today. I was shooing brothers out of the way, checking the light, and setting up for classic, moody B & W photos. One shot and my shutter jammed . . . me cussing, Barry and the guys still rapping . . . "That's gotta be the ugliest piano going, our piano . . . do you really think Dylan might have played it?"

Dinkytown had perked up; Friday afternoon in the university community was working its magic, people rushed up and down the block, ducking into restaurants, campus hangouts, and liquor stores, getting ready, getting ready . . . I pulled my Powr-House Blue Denim Engineer's cap down over my eyes and hoped I wouldn't run into David Zimmerman.

My goddamn camera was broken—it wouldn't cock, and the shutter refused to move. That was just great. My only hope was to somehow get the thing repaired before Echo and I took off for Hibbing, but that was less than an hour away now; the one shop on Fourth Street I had already tried told me the job would take several days, and be expensive. Joy. Naturally, I had *lots* of money to spare. I had barely enough to get home right now, let alone to allow for an extended stay in the north country. Shit. I decided to ride it on out with a chocolate soda at Gray's Drugstore.

That picked me up. I sat at the ancient soda fountain for a good forty-five minutes, copying my notes on Ellen Baker, and musing about Dinkytown. Thank goodness I'd gotten a *few* pictures. You couldn't really describe Dinkytown, the whole scene was so typical; you had to see a photo. Hibbing was different, the north country was different—I longed to get back up there—but Minneapolis . . . one could imagine F. Scott Fitzgerald pacing its dull streets, dreaming of heading back to Princeton. And Dylan, lusting for New York in such a similar fashion. The parallel between the two writers didn't seem strained here at Gray's. New York was just as much Dylan's "splendid mirage" as his fellow Minnesotan's, and if *Highway 61, Revisited* wasn't Dylan's version of Fitzgerald's *Crack-Up,* then I hadn't been through all of F. Scott Fitzgerald's books. Or sat at his grave in Rockville, Maryland...yes, Scott's buried there, just fifteen minutes from my house. Although he was born in Minnesota, Scott's ancestors were from Maryland. He hadn't been named Francis Scott Key Fitzgerald in jest. My family had quite a Maryland heritage itself, and perhaps that was one of the reasons I felt so close to Scott. Little girls left notes scribbled on looseleaf notebook paper at his gravesite—"Dear Scott...loved your books." I probably spent more time in Scott's graveyard than was healthy, but...anyway, all of it came back now, here in Dinkytown, tracking down Dylan's past, waiting to see Echo again...I paid the lady behind the counter and split.

Outside, the evening wafted in like summer-in-the-city; you could smell *everything,* feel the pavement tingle like an asphalt basketball court lit up for a record hop, taste beer in the backseats of '57 Chevys, touch nylon and imitation cashmere at the bodice of the day. I cocked my hat back on my head—daring fate and David Zimmerman—and whipped into a newsstand. They sold the *Village Voice!* My series had finished two weeks ago, but...yep, a review of *Nashville Skyline,* by Robert Christgau. With: "A new version of Dylan is emerging, if not from Toby Thompson's recent *Voice* series, then from Dylan himself...." The kid puffed right up, thought about offering his clerk an autograph, but turned to a book review by Richard Goldstein instead. It was a charming putdown of Rudolph Wurlitzer's novel, *Nog:* "Better you should sow your oats in the post-war novel, than pollute the New Journalism, where Mailer and Yurick and the poets over at St. Mark's in the Bouwerie have deserted the new consciousness...." You tell 'em Richard. I suddenly felt a part of it all. The *Village Voice* was exactly what you needed in Minnesota, a half hour before you picked up the "Girl from the North Country." There was a stack of old, sun-yellowed and well-read *Voices* behind the counter, and I asked if I might take a look. *Natch.* They had a copy of the "Echo" part of my story, with the front-page headline, DYLAN'S NORTH COUNTRY GIRL, PG. 33 staring out at the world. The lady gave it to me, and I stuffed it into my pocket for Echo.

GUSHICON FIVE: *Lookin' to Get Silly*

"Turn that part up!" she squealed, as I eased off the Highway 65 into the parking lot beside Dibbo's Diner. "I love it when they break into that heavy rhythm. I wrote a junior high school term paper on music like that. Colored jazz with a big beat. They wouldn't let me write on rock and roll. *That* wasn't a fit subject, my music teacher said. Hibbing is so hokey; to this day, I get the funniest feeling whenever I go back."

Echo was dressed in knee-high white boots, black minidress, and Austrian cape, and she was sitting beside me in the front seat of my Volkswagen, with her blue eyes, baggage—dresses and slacks and things, just tossed in the back—huge funky sunglasses and ash-blond hair, right there, *in my car,* and here we were in Mora, Minnesota, a halfway stop on the road to Hibbing, at a trucker's café near the Snake River, where I would get out on my side of the car, walk around to open her door, help her out, lock it up—all that wonderful stuff—and we would have coffee.

No, hot chocolate; and Echo couldn't stop. "Bob was a lot luckier with his teachers. He had that nice Mrs. Peterson in music, for one thing, and that made all the difference in the world. The woman *I* had practically ruined my life. That whole eleventh-grade year when Bob and I went steady, he had the music teachers snowed. Hardly anybody else could stand how he sung or what he played—especially the electric stuff—but people like Mrs. Peterson and

Bob's English teacher, Mr. Rolfzen, they had a feeling. Bob would play for anyone, anytime, and I guess that made a difference, too. He was such a sweet convincer. But *me* . . . ooh, that music teacher!"

People were staring. *People,* not just truck drivers, were staring at Echo and me in our funny clothes and funky manner, but Echo didn't seem to care, even though they were looking at her the most, 'cause she looked pretty lookable. I was getting those stares I always got in places like this.

Echo tossed her head and met a few eyeballs. "Yes, we're back in the sticks again. Home Sweet Home, for a north country weekend. They'll talk behind your back, but they can't look you in the eye. Just a *little* different, that's all you have to be. They make me so mad, it's the same as when I was a kid in Hibbing, they'd never leave me alone. Oh, I was a sexy little thing; you should have seen me in my first pair of leopard-skin pants, if you don't think that shook 'em up on Howard Street!"

Oh. Yes.

"You'd *better* be able to get your camera fixed in Hibbing 'cause I brought some great things to wear." She laughed. We had tried to have my camera repaired at several stores in Minneapolis, but none could do the job right away. No. They couldn't. I'd *buy* a camera, a goddamned Nikon on credit if I had to.

"I guess the main reason Bob and I got along so well was 'cause we were both so wild. But I was a lot wilder than him at first; I suppose I sort of changed him some. But not much, his craziness had always been there; it just needed somebody to bring it out. I sure was that somebody. Even after we broke up, I did nutty things, and I was older then! Like right after graduation, my girlfriend and I hit the road—literally. We hitchhiked *all over* the place, and you know girls weren't doing that the way they are now. We had some adventures! We camped out and slept in parks. Met other crazies like us and traveled together. It was a lot like what Bob always wanted to do, and like the fibs he told on the back of his first album . . . that stuff about traveling with a circus. Bob never did anything like that, at least not that I ever heard of. His weird

imagination! But *I* sure did all that stuff, spent most of my graduation summer doing it. And in Minneapolis, too; that was *really* scary.
But we got through it somehow, my girlfriend and me." Echo
drained the last of her cocoa, and folded up her purse. "What do
you say we get out of here, this place gives me the creeps."

Outside of Dibbo's the wind had kicked up, and one of those
north-country sunsets I'd been thinking about for ten months was
slinking sensuously across the horizon. And that chill, a stiff, northern Minnesota reminder that the sun was going down . . . I pulled
the heater lever on my VW up full, and labored the engine in third
gear for three-quarters of a mile.

Echo was reading about herself in the *Village Voice*. "How did
you remember all this stuff, Toby? When I told it to you I never
dreamed I'd be so big a part of your story. A whole section!"

I turned toward her smiling, and a semi almost blew us off the
road. Stupid Highway 65 was only two lanes wide, and everybody
hauled.

"Oh, I never said this . . . this is funny, I can't believe you wrote
it. I guess your memory isn't as good as I thought, huh?"

"Which, where?"

"This story about Bob coming over to my house with his guitar,
and singing 'Do You Want to Dance,' that's not right. He called me
up one time and played it over the telephone, the actual record,
but he didn't sing it for my parents or anything."

"I must have dreamt it that way, I suppose. It's a good story
though, I'm glad I have it in there. Sounds like something Bob
might have done."

"You're worse than he was, I swear. But . . . you know what actually did happen that time? He called me like I said, but told me it
was *him* singing. He was always making tapes with his band, so
naturally I believed him. I even complimented him on how much
they'd improved. Was a *long* time afterward that I realized it wasn't
Bob and the band, but Bobby Freeman. Spooky stuff."

Sounded pretty straight to me. Dylan could be Bobby Freeman
for all I knew, but my theory was that Bob and Smokey Robinson

were the same. If you've ever seen Smokey and the Miracles, I'm certain you'll agree without a moment's hesitation. And if you haven't, just think about it: Up there on that stage before a five-piece soul band, with the essence of black vocal accompaniment at his side—plus, I grant you, a little makeup, his hair slicked back, some Man Tan, and a puff or two of cotton in the nostrils—is Bobby Zimmerman, luxuriating in the apotheosis of his '57 Jacket Jamboree Talent Festival performance. There was no doubt in my mind, Bob Dylan *was* Smokey Robinson. And I had evidence to support my belief: Smokey uses a quote from Bob in his program notes that says, "Smokey Robinson is today's greatest living American poet." Without reservation. And all one really has to do, if still unconvinced, is listen to the Miracles' songs . . . numbers like "The Tracks of My Tears," "The Love I Saw in You Was Just a Mirage," or "More Love." *Nobody* but Bob could have written the lines:

> This is no fiction, this is no fact,
> This is real,
> It's a pact . . .

Imagine how much *fun* Bob has being Smokey Robinson. No stupid reporters questioning the literacy of his work, no phony image of Pop Seer to live up to. Nothing but *soul*—and those slick clothes and that *big* beat. Bob didn't really spend two years and a half brooding in Woodstock, he was on the road with the Miracles!

"Toby . . ."

"Huh? Oh, I'm sorry, I must have been dreaming." Too little sleep, too many hours on the road, and too much happening. "What was it you were saying?"

Echo waved a letter under my nose. "This. I thought you might be interested in seeing it; it's from Robert Shelton."

"Wow, *yes,* what does he say? Read it to me."

"Oh, not much. Except that if he can consider his interview with me exclusive, there will be more than the enclosed one hundred dollar check coming, when and if his book starts to make money."

"He sent you a hundred dollars?" I asked.

"Yeah, and I guess I really blew it by talking to you, didn't I?" Echo laughed.

"Gosh . . ."

"I'm only kidding, what do I care? It's more fun having you write about Bob, anyhow."

"Well, that's good, because I'm sure not going to be able to give you a hundred bucks. That's *amazing*. He must be getting a lot of bread from somebody to be throwing it around like that. Some publisher, I mean." Oh, empty-pocketed gloom.

"Cheer up, he's a nice fellow. He won't be mad. And besides, it was all my fault. I never actually thought you'd get your story published. I just figured you were one of Bob's fans who was interested enough in his music to come all the way to Minnesota. That's why I talked to you; I never even thought about you being any competition for Robert Shelton."

"I sure can't say I blame you for that." Echo flashed me a grin and turned back to her *Voice*. We drove along in silence for five or ten miles, her reading and me watching the road, all pale pink and Christmas-tree green in the dusk. It was really getting cold now, and I shivered with the heat up full, in my chamois-cloth lumberjack shirt and heavy wool socks. Echo huddled in her Austrian cape under the overhead light. I thought seriously of breaking out the Scotch that was bouncing around in my glove compartment.

"Ooh, Toby . . . I bet Bob's wife didn't like all *this*."

"What's that?" I said, my teeth chattering.

"This stuff about us wanting to get married—I bet that just made her furious."

"Come on, you were two kids in love, of course you talked about getting married. Everybody does. Don't you think Bob Dylan's *wife* would understand something as normal as that?" Echo looked up hurt.

"Well, all I know is that we seemed pretty serious at the time. He even made me cook *pizzas* for him to prove I'd be a good wife, and once I had to sew a pair of blue slacks—best sewing job I ever did!"

I started laughing; I couldn't help it, but I did. Echo just stared. "That's funny, *pizzas...*" I gulped. Echo sort of smiled and then giggled. "And blue slacks," she whispered, "royal blue slacks, I'll never forget them." She looked up at me and laughed.

"That's better, oh god, I need a drink." I uncorked the pint of Cutty Sark and offered Echo a snort.

"No thanks!" she said, looking mildly shocked. I took a long pull and stuck the bottle in my coat pocket.

"You *are* crazy." She laughed again.

"I'm a *in*-sane," the Cutty Sark roared. "And, 'Sometimes, I might get drunk... walk like a duck, and smell like a skunk...'"

"Oh, hush. And keep your eyes on the road!" Another semi blasted by and almost launched us into a very large body of water. The bottle of Scotch quickly found its way to my mouth. "Pull off here for a minute," Echo said. "There, that side road."

I did as ordered and eased off Highway 65 into a small unpaved parking lot. "This is Big Sandy Lake." Echo sighed. "See now? Isn't that neat?"

I pulled up the hand brake, wiped off the windshield with a sleeve of my shirt, and gazed out onto the most beautifully moonscaped water I had ever seen. The lake flapped and flopped out for a mile or so, to tremendous northern pines of exactly the right height— their shaggy tops extending to tickle the breast of a moon so angry and red that it hissed across the black-green water like some carelessly ignited railroad flare. The radio was playing something appropriate, from someplace like Fort Wayne, Indiana, and we were less than an hour from Hibbing. Echo and I sat in our seats, just staring. It was, well...

"I always did like to stop here," Echo finally said.

"You don't want to go over to your mother's yet, do you?" I said. "It's only ten thirty. And Friday night. How about seeing what's happening at the Garden Lounge; maybe they have a band tonight? Huh?" We had just swung onto Howard Street, at the east end of town. Things didn't seem to have changed much;

I certainly felt no different—different, yes, from the first time I drove down Hibbing's main street but unchanged in that I felt I'd been away, oh, a week or two at the most. I was clearly playing host to Echo—it seemed as if I knew the place better than she.

"The *Garden Lounge.*" She beamed. "I haven't been there in years. They never used to have bands; that's incredible, are you sure?"

"They had bands last time I was out. But I'm not certain about Friday nights. We can try, though."

"OK, that might be fun!"

We found a place to park my car on crowded Howard Street and shivered across to our destination. They had a band all right, you could hear it halfway down the block. But once inside . . . what was this? Sounds of *hard rock* drifting through the smoke of old miners' cigars, "Sunshine of Your Love" blasting loose cobwebs of iron ore dust and saloon perfume, kids with long hair, bellbottoms, and ankle-high boots on the bandstand . . . and people tolerating it! What's more, dancing to it!

"I haven't heard anything like this in Hibbing since Bob and I used to stay up late for Gatemouth Page's radio show," Echo shouted in my ear. "They never had groups like this before, *anyplace.*"

We found a table, ordered, and sat back in awe of an Iron Butterfly tune the band had just started. "They couldn't be from *Hibbing,*" I stammered.

"What do you mean, 'couldn't be from Hibbing,'" Echo laughed. "Bob's from Hibbing!"

She had me there. But the change was staggering. People on the dance floor didn't look so different, but this band . . . I decided to tempt the inevitable.

"I'm going to ask them if they know any of Bob's songs," I screamed at Echo, "excuse me for a minute." The lead guitarist had just finished a solo, so I approached him. Nope, of course not, but they could handle one or two Donovan numbers.

I shook my head NO at Echo and sat back down. She had already finished her Tom Collins, and I was three-quarters of the way through my Grain Belt Premium, so I ordered us both another. The band screamed their set to a halt with "Satisfaction," and Echo leaned a little closer.

"Did I tell you about the song I wrote the other day? After you called and said you were coming back out to Minnesota—plus all the stuff you and everybody else have been writing about Bob lately, the magazine covers, his album staring at me from windows of all the record stores . . . did I tell you about it?"

"Christ, no! Let's hear it."

"Oh, there's no music . . . except that I thought maybe it could be played like one of Bob's old talking blues."

"Recite it then!"

"Oh, I couldn't do that! Here, someplace . . . here, I have it written down." Echo shoved a dirty white envelope in front of me, with her scribbling up and down and around the entire surface. I couldn't read it, not for the life of me.

"You're going to have to," I said. "I can't piece the thing together."

"All right, but don't laugh." Echo cleared her throat and began, reciting her lyrics carefully in that cute little-girl voice. "It's about Bob."

> *First you come around*
> *With your singing and dancing*
> *Wild hair waving, and fancy-pantsing*
> *And you want to be seen!*
>
> *So the people came from miles around*
> *Just to see you smile*
> *And laugh and frown*
> *Like a crazy clown*
> *With your hair hanging down!*
>
> *Now you've left town.*
> *Don't want nobody hanging round.*
> *You wanna hide*
> *Won't go outside*
> *Don't make the scene*
> *You don't wanna be seen.*
>
> *I think you're mean!*

"That's great"—I applauded—"what do you call it, I mean do you have a title yet?"

"I only just wrote it the other day." Echo was very excited.

"Why don't you call it, 'Boy from the North Country'?"

She caught my teasing and smiled. "Oh, Bob probably wouldn't like that at *all*."

"We'll try it to music later," I hollered. The band had started. "I have my guitar in the car... and harmonica!" I was getting drunk, too. What the hell, I ordered two more.

"Come on," Echo screamed, grabbing my hand. "Let's dance!"

DÉJÀGUSH I: *Woke in the Mornin' Wonderin'*

"No," I protested, "no, don't tell me . . . really?"

"Uh-huh"—Echo smiled over her tomato juice—"just after the band broke into their polka number. You stood on your head right there in the middle of the dance floor, and everybody moved back and cheered. All the change fell out of your pockets, and your keys, and somebody came up later with your traveler's checks, but you didn't seem to care. It was fun."

Oh god. "Hit me with all of it, come on, there must be more."

"Well, afterward, you weren't anywhere near ready to stop, so we drove up to Chisholm. Nothing was happening there either, so we found you that room at Michael's Motel, and you insisted on playing the guitar. Woke up the whole place, I think. People were beating on walls . . ."

"With the harmonica too, I suppose?"

"Sure. It was loud, but boy, did it ever sound neat! You sang 'Girl from the North Country' for me and some other songs—they were real good. How come you sound so much like Bob?"

"Yeah, I remember 'Girl from the North Country.'" I cringed. "I'll never forget it . . . and what you said when I finished."

"Oh, Toby . . ."

"Oh, Toby, nothing! Here I was, twelve hundred miles from home, at the end of my quest, Dylan's north country muse at my side, his tribute to her slipping off my tongue . . ."

"Listen to him now!"

". . . guitar in hand, harmonica softly wailing, finish the song, and what is her comment . . . *Feel better now?* What a put-down!"

"It wasn't like that at all"—Echo giggled—"you just didn't realize I was teasing." Echo cut her pancakes and poured syrup onto each little pile.

"Oh, I realized, believe me, I realized. *Feel better now?* Served me right, I suppose." I took a bite of my Denver sandwich and almost gagged. Breakfast at the Sportsmen's Café . . . not all it might have been, under different circumstances. I glanced around the room, searching for familiar faces. Ten o'clock Saturday morning didn't breed many. I hoped I wouldn't run into Don McKenzie—paranoia struck deep. Well, back to work.

"Did you and Bob ever hang out here?" I asked. Echo sopped up some syrup with a sausage link and cut it daintily.

"Of course, this was one of our regular spots. We'd come in for Cokes and hamburgers all the time. As a matter of fact, we used to sit in this booth . . . either here or the opposite one at the back. Just about always."

I moved uneasily in my seat. "I just remembered about my camera. Where are we going to get it fixed?"

"I know a couple of places; and don't worry, we'll find you another if yours is finished. I think one of Bob's cousins rents them, up at Stein's Drugstore."

"Come on then, the light's pretty good, and there's no sense in wasting any more of it than we have to." Echo was still eating, but she wiped her mouth and shoved her plate aside. I wasn't being very polite, but god, what a headache. My fault, I know. I paid the cashier, and we hustled out onto Howard Street. At least it was a nice spring day, warm and all that.

We tried every camera store in town, four, I believe, and not one could fix the thing in a day. So, off to Stein's—Bob's cousin all right, who said yes, he might be able to rent me a camera, but I'd have to come back later. To give him time to check me out? I don't know, but by two o'clock I had a $199 Kodak Instamatic, and Echo and I were strolling up Saturday afternoon's Howard Street at last.

Past . . . the old L & B, which was now a flower shop, Crippa's, Bob's old music headquarters, and Collier's Barbeque, off on a side street, and now the R & S Café—closed, and for rent.

"Right there," Echo was saying, "in that corner, is where Bob and his band used to play. Collier's would let them come in on week-ends most anytime they wanted to, and they'd move those booths away from the window here, and face the back of the room. They were so loud you could hear them all the way up the block! Like I told you, Bob always had his amplifiers too high."

I moved across the street and took a few shots. Echo looked extra good this morning, in some sort of slack-suit getup, with ruffled sleeves and a high collar. We walked on up the street and paused at an archaic red calliope—Kitchen's Kitchenette—where appar-ently she, Bob, and every other kid who has grown up in Hibbing have, at one time or another, bought candy bars, cotton candy, or ten-cent bags of popcorn.

"Do you want some popcorn, Echo?"

"Sure. We can share!" The girl in the little wagon scooped out a bag of the best, and I snapped a few more shots of Echo before we moved on . . . up Howard Street, through Saturday afternoon crowds of shoppers, kids gunning motors and screaming at each other from slick hot rods, loiterers commenting on Echo's and my strange ap-pearances—"See what I mean, Toby, they can't tolerate anything different, and they always have something mean to say. *Ooh*, they make me mad! I've never had a moment's peace in this town."

All of a sudden she grabbed my hand and started pulling me across the street—horns honking, people screaming. "What are you doing?" I panted. Echo was tossing her hair and sort of hopping back and forth. "I don't know, does there have to be a reason?"

"Hell no!" I laughed, and we busted on down the street.

"See that lamppost there?" Echo said. "Right there in front of the Moose Lodge? That's where I first met Bob. Well, it was in the L & B afterward really, but there on that corner was where I first noticed him. How could I help it! Like I told you, he was standing in the middle of the sidewalk, playing the guitar and singing, and it must have been ten o'clock at night. He and the band had been rehearsing upstairs in the Moose Lodge, and they were going into the L & B. Oh, but look at it now . . . it's gone! Why did they do *that?*"

Echo pressed her nose against the window of the flower shop and pointed with a chubby finger. I was taking pictures like crazy. "That's where Bob came over to talk with me, he and his friend, John Bucklen." Echo wiped off the wet spot left by her nose on the glass and stood back. "Bob was *so* cocky. Right from the beginning . . . but after we started going together, we'd walk up Howard Street, just like you and I are doing now, Bob in those tight jeans he wore, with his hands squeezed into the pockets as far as he could get them, and he'd drag me into Crippa's or one of the other stores which sold records. He'd walk up to the clerk like that in those jeans and with that kooky little grin, and ask for some record he *knew* they wouldn't have. The clerk would say, 'Little Who?' or 'Fats What?' and Bob would say, 'Well, how 'bout such and such— or so and so's new one?' and the clerk would never even have *heard* of them, let alone have the records. Bob would keep that up until the clerk was just about furious, and then Bob'd put on his hurt look and we'd leave, him almost ready to burst from not laughing."

Shades of brother David. We were at the corner of Fifth Avenue and Howard, near Zimmerman's. "What about Bob and his father's shop—did he ever have to work there or anything; did he ever talk about that sort of stuff with you?"

"Oh, it's right down that street, too," Echo said, looking vaguely frightened. "I never go in there anymore, not at all. My mother tells me they're going out of business, you know; after almost twenty-five years, here and in Duluth. Too much new competition, I guess. Sure, Bob's father used to make him do odd jobs around the shop, and he'd tell me about it afterward. He and this other fellow sometimes would have to go out on a truck and repossess stuff. I think that's where Bob first started feeling sorry for poor people. These miners would come to town, find a house, buy furniture on the credit their job promised them, and then get laid off when a mine shut down. Mining was a terrible gamble in those days. It's not so bad now with the taconite process . . . but anyway, then Bob and his friend would have to go over and take away all the stuff bought from Zimmerman's. Load it onto the truck and just leave. Bob hated that—used to dread it worse than anything."

"I guess so. I can't imagine anybody enjoying that sort of job." Echo was pulling me across the street again. "Hey though, what about going by and saying hello to old Maurice Zimmerman? I'd like to see him and find out if he read the story; after all, he *was* my primary motivation in coming out here."

"*No,*" Echo said, looking scared again, "you go ahead if you want to. I can't go in there, I'd be embarrassed."

"Echo . . ."

"No really, if you want to go, go ahead. I'll meet you in Sammy's Pizza Palace."

"OK, if you insist; don't worry, though, I won't be long."

GUSHICON SIX: *The Sonuvabitch Never Had No Religion*

Zimmerman's was still there all right, its pale pink presence stood out over Fifth Avenue like some once-glamorous toilet fixture in a recently remodeled bathroom. The Kay Hotel still advertised rooms for rent overhead; but inside, the main showroom was almost empty. One or two big appliances sat obscenely in the middle of the floor, flanked by packing crates, tarpaulins, and little piles of swept-up debris. Paul Zimmerman was behind the counter, and he seemed to recognize me as soon as I walked in.

I reintroduced myself and asked about his brother Maurice, who apparently was home—it being Saturday, the store wasn't officially open for business—and Paul chatted amiably with me for several minutes. He hadn't seen the story himself, but others had, and he'd heard the talk. No, people weren't upset really, just talkative. Paul smiled. I asked if what I'd heard from Echo was true, that the store was going out of business, and Paul's smile turned in on itself, laughing, as if at somebody else's joke. Yes, Paul answered, with a shrug of his shoulders. After twenty-five years, too. Well, businesses open and close all the time . . . Would he and Maurice reopen anyplace else? No, Paul didn't think so.

I asked about Bob's mother, how she was doing, and whether or not she was back in town—Paul said he thought she was in Minneapolis now with David and Gail. Great, I thought, she'll hear wonderful things about me from them. And get a chance to read what I'd written on David, the only section of my *Voice* piece I felt really guilty about (except for the part where Bob says that awful stuff about Joan Baez's picture—why did I write those two things? they were true, sure, but they probably hurt ... I don't know). Paul told me to call Bob's aunt; she'd know more of what Mrs. Zimmerman's schedule was. He puffed on his cigar and looked disinterested.

I thought of buying something but couldn't imagine what. A toaster, a flashlight? No, I had better just leave. I shook hands with Paul Zimmerman and asked him to be sure and say hello to Maurice for me. Paul smiled again and said he would. I looked around the shop once more and shuffled on over to the door, dreaming of other footsteps on the same tile, in different dust, but sharing, perhaps, the same sadness at leaving. *But then,* the doorbell jingled, *maybe not.* You certainly couldn't say for sure, not about that or anything else in Hibbing. Not about people, anyway. Not about affection. Love?

DÉJÀGUSH II: *Jimmy Brown the Newsboy*

I had met Echo at Sammy's as planned, but Cokes and a small anchovies-and-mushroom hadn't sounded right; so now we were enjoying our second Grain Belt Premium in the Jolly Rodger Café, down at the east end of Howard Street. Old miners with Powr-House Blue Denim Engineer's caps, heavy olive-drab jackets, and high-top boots were drinking and talking in hoarse roars. The Wilburn Brothers picked a lively number from the ancient, half-converted nickelodeon in the corner; there was a pool game going on just this side of the bar; and the cussing of two old-timers at a back-room card table knifed through the din.

Echo tossed her long hair, took a bite from her hot dog and a pull on her beer. I was still quiet from my Zimmerman's experience, and Echo seemed edgy, overly gay in her attempts to lighten my mood.

"Bob and I used to love to eat hot dogs," she said, with a lilt in her voice, "not like this one, *ugh,* but like we got out on the road to my house. At the A & W rootbeer stand. He'd always make me buy him hot dogs—with mustard and relish. He'd say, 'Please Echo, please, I'm *starving,*' and we'd have to stop. He never seemed to have any money. I actually think I had more spending money than he did. So *I* usually bought the hot dogs. He'd give me a bite. It was the same thing the one or two times I saw him in Minneapolis. I can remember having to buy him turkey and peanut butter sandwiches at the Scholar. Oof! Didn't want a bite of those."

I smiled slightly and signaled the waitress for two more beers. Echo looked encouraged.

"We'd usually pull into the Hibbing rootbeer stand on Bob's motorcycle . . . when the weather was warm, that is. One time, just outside my house on the old service road, he tried to teach me how to ride it. He told me all about the controls, started it up, and set me onboard. Only trouble was that my feet weren't long enough to reach the ground; but I didn't realize that until I'd already taken off. I made it about twenty yards in first gear and thought I'd better practice stopping before I went any further, so I tried to put on the brakes; but something went wrong and the engine started revving and I hit a post or a tree and went head over heels. The motorcycle fell over and the rear wheel went crazy with sparks flying and gravel . . . Bob stood there with his mouth open and his eyes real big, not believing it." I laughed and poured her a glass of beer.

"Another time, after school one day, he came over to my house just pale as a ghost. He said he'd hit a little kid with his motorcycle. Apparently he hadn't hurt the little kid, but it scared Bob to death. He'd had to go down to the police station and everything. He sold his motorcycle the next day."

Up at the bar, an old fellow in a worn hunting vest and dayglored deer cap, exploded in a fit of rage, damning and threatening some invisible foe. God, Hitler, and the Third Division suffered heavy casualties; and in the wake of their siege I could feel Echo move a little closer beside me in our booth. One or two of the oldtimer's barmates casually looked up . . . returning to their beers. The area remained under attack for several minutes, but the old warrior's barrage finally subsided into a flood of gesticulated beer and damp mutterings.

"That sort of thing used to happen all the *time* up here." Echo shuddered, her hand on my arm. "These old miners, some of them don't have many brains left. I'd be so glad when Bob was there."

"Come on, if it scares you," I said. "Let's get outside."

Back on Howard Street, Echo and I stopped into various shops. At Crippa's, the saleslady who had sold Bob his first harmonica rack recognized me and offered a haughty hello. She hadn't seen my story, but one of her friends had, and told Saleslady she wouldn't have liked it. But Chet Crippa was smiling and friendly, and invited me to stop by tomorrow for coffee; and I noticed *Nashville Skyline* was in stock, had its own special section, and the Milton Glaser "Dylan" poster glowered from a prominent spot toward the rear of the store.

Up at Team Electronics—one of Zimmerman's new competitors—Echo did a suspicious-looking hop and pulled me to a halt. "Toby, I just had a great idea! You know my song, the one I wrote for Bob?"

"Sure."

"Well. I was thinking maybe we could record it, you know, make a tape and try to send it to Bob. You could play your guitar, and I'd sing!"

"That's a great idea . . . if we can find somebody with a recorder."

"Here's a whole storeful!" Echo said, pointing at Team's big picture window.

"It's worth a try, I suppose." So I hiked back to the car, picked up my instruments, Echo turned on her north country smile, and we conned Joe Hyduke at Team Electronics into setting up a miniature recording studio, four-track stereo, monitors ("Uh, we were wondering how much you'd charge to record a song for us, with her singing, and me playing the guitar." Joe looks at me and my guitar; Joe looks at Echo, at Echo, at Echo . . . "I wouldn't charge you nothing!"), right there in the front of the store. Customers are incredulous. Two blond crazies, one playing this corny, country-style guitar with a harmonica chunka-chunking along at the same time, and the other bouncing around and warbling in a Brigitte Bardot, baby-girl voice, that great song: "First you come around with your singing and dancing, your wild hair waving, and fancy-pantsing . . ."

Finish to applause; fade to Joe and Toby and Echo back at the Garden Lounge, lubing up for cocktail hour. Joe tells Toby about Hibbing and Hibbing and a little more Hibbing, interspersed with slaps on the back and calls to the bartender for "another round." Joe tells Toby about a tiny coffee house discothèque David Zimmerman had run for a while, just around the corner, called the Escape à Go-Go. It had been open for about a year and a half, serving near-beer; Joe thought Bob's money had been behind it. Joe suggests to Toby and Echo that they take their tape over to Hibbing's radio station—maybe they'd play it over the air? Toby and Echo thank Joe and agree. They leave him sitting at the bar of the Garden Lounge, a less-bored young man.

"It's amazing how much you sound like Bob!" Echo was saying. "I mean, I realize you've listened to his records a lot, but the similarity is more than just that; it's weird!"

Yes, well. "Where do I turn now, Echo?"

"Ooh, *there,* I almost forgot about telling you. It's like you should know or something. Bob and I used to come out here, and . . . well, he would play the tapes *he'd* made."

WMFG, Hibbing's 1000-watt giant, is situated in a poor section of the village, surrounded by tumble-down shacks with raggedy Indian kids peeking out from behind unpainted porch posts, and flanked by open country almost to the mines. We parked my car out front and breezed through the open screen door. Eighteen-year-old Bob Stehlin was the DJ on duty, and we caught him plugged into his own cassette recordings of contemporary rock, while a taped "how to make a dress" show played over the air.

Ron Marinelli, the old station director and fellow who used to play Bob's tapes, was no longer with the station. Ron had been interested in Bob and his band, Bob Stehlin told me, and would probably have stories to tell . . . but he wasn't around anymore . . . Bob Stehlin wasn't sure but thought he might be program director at a station over in Virginia. Bob Stehlin didn't remember ever having heard Bob or his tapes in the Hibbing days, but was excited about playing the tape Echo and I had made at Team's. But . . . the speed was wrong. Bob Stehlin decided he wanted an interview anyway, so we consented to do Echo's song live . . . After my interview, a long pompous thing, with me quoting everyone from Walt Whitman to Jack Newfield, and promising respect the world over for Hibbing's forgotten Dylanites. Christ! But Echo's song . . . tremendous. She sang it like a trooper (first calling her mother to be sure all the relatives were listening), and my backup work wasn't any slouch-shit either...I really *was* sounding more and more like Dylan. And as for our radio audience, smash success! Telephones ringing, *who in the world do you have out there?*...Bob Stehlin followed up with an entire side of *Dylan's Greatest Hits*, probably more Bob than Hibbing had heard since the man left town.

Echo and I caught our breath as Bob Stehlin waited for the record to run out, and listened halfheartedly while he told us a bit about himself and his job at WMFG. "We're definitely a middle of the road station...you know, little old ladies who have been listening to the same music for forty-five years, and who have no intention of changing. So we don't play much Dylan. But I'm crazy about his music. He seems to have transcended acid-rock and all that; he puts things simply enough in his music so that you can understand what's happening. Not that what he has to say is simple, but at least the medium gives you a chance. I think a lot of the kids around Hibbing these days feel the same way. They're learning to appreciate and to be proud of Dylan."

"Last fall when I was here, I was hard-pressed to find anybody who would say he even liked Bob's music, let alone someone who claimed to be proud of it."

"Well, nine or ten months has made quite a bit of difference. You've probably noticed that more long hair and hippy-influenced fashions have cropped up, as well." Bob Stehlin looked over at Echo and smiled. "I sure hope there'll be a corresponding boom in modern thought patterns. Actually, I think there already is."

"Have you ever met Dylan?" I asked.

"No, but last time he was in town—for his father's funeral, I guess—a bunch of us saw him up on Howard Street. He was on this big hairy Triumph, parked at the curb; he was just sitting there, smoking a *huge* cigar, and eyeing people as they walked by. Too much!"

Echo and I were having drinks in the pre-atmosphered Pub Room of the Kahler Inn Towne Motel. I was jotting a few of the day's happenings in my notebook, while the very last of the Hibbing High School track meet flickered on the Pub Room's big color TV. Echo was chattering along, but I wasn't paying too much attention. I stared off into the corner of the Pub Room's stand-up-or-sit-down bar where I'd had my first Hibbing drink with Don McKenzie the previous fall. The same little knickknacks hovered behind bottles, and a carefully constructed, plastic mixer-stick something still reflected in the Pub Room's big mirror. They were getting ready to turn off the television because Johnny the piano player had arrived; people were trickling in for cocktails. Echo glanced up at the TV.

"Now *that's* something they never used to do . . . broadcast high school athletic events over the television station. Hibbing sure is coming up in the world. Bob would really have laughed if he could have seen that."

Johnny the piano player had his red blazer on, and the bartender walked over to shut off the TV. In the several minutes between the time the TV's sound died and Johnny started his first number, the drone of Muzak could be heard from another room.

"You hear that song!"—Echo shuddered—"the one they're playing over the speakers? Do you recognize it?"

I listened for a moment and had to confess that I didn't. It was standard, mid-fifties, C, A-Minor, F, G-Seventh arrangement, I knew that much.

"It's 'Angel Baby.'" Echo moaned. "Bob used to call me that . . . Angel Baby, I mean."

"For Christ's sake," I said. "I'm taking you home."

GUSHICON SEVEN: *Contacts Among the Lumberjacks, Shouting the Word "Now"*

Echo and I had both enjoyed a good night's sleep, and spirits were up this bright Sunday morning. My Volkswagen bounced over the road, and a fine spray of red colored our wake. We were off to North Hibbing for a picture-taking session; Echo was leaving her mother's to go back to Minneapolis that evening, and I was staying on at Michael's Motel until I completed my piece for *US*. I was working under a deadline, after all.

I pulled the car to a stop in front of a crumbling wall toward the center of the old town. Echo hopped out and took a look, turning over pieces of rubble with her toe. "I *think* this is it, Toby. I'm not completely certain, but I *think* so. It's been so long since I was up here. None of these other buildings look like they'd have been big enough for a courthouse, but you can't really tell anymore. Maybe that one . . ."

Echo pointed off about thirty yards to the east, at half a chimney. "No," I said, "I doubt whether the courthouse would have had a brick chimney. It was stone structure after all, according to Bob, anyway."*

"Oh, I don't know." Echo frowned. "I just can't remember."

We got back into the car and drove on around to the mining offices, up at the northwest end of town.

---

* Liner notes to *The Times They Are A-Changin'*.

No private buildings were left, just the company's official shack—an arena-sized affair, encircled by a tall Anchor fence. Echo and I just sat, staring at the building's hulk, listening to WEBC from Duluth, and sipping coffee we'd brought from the Sportsmen's.

"Isn't there a regular mine-viewing site around here someplace?" I asked. "Seems I've noticed it advertised."

Echo brightened, "Wanna go see it?"

"I thought all that was closed, except for the summer?"

"It is, but come on ... who cares?"

We walked around the far side of the mining shack, still drinking our coffee, and came to a fairly high barbed-wire fence. I stopped and looked up at the No Trespassing sign. "Echo, maybe we'd ..."

"Follow me," she said, scrambling up a pole and over the wire in a moment. I shrugged and buttoned my jacket, hoping I might possess half her grace in the effort. The gods were with me, and I dropped without incident into the mud on the other side.

We walked on down a narrow dirt road for several hundred yards, until Echo veered into the grass ... toward another fence, I was unhappy to notice. She vaulted it with similar ease, and beckoned me to follow. We raced up a fifty-foot gravel embankment to the gray snake of an idle ore train.

"Come on, slowpoke!" she teased. "The mines are just on the other side!"

"How are we going to get around that train?"

"Watch," she said, and slipped out of sight between two cars.

"Echo!" But she was on the coupling mechanism and carefully inching her way under and around machinery. She knew what she was doing; I moaned, but my pride and will to follow were too strong for common sense. I hopped aboard ... Great Northern, Rock Island Line.

At the other side ... there it was, the end of the world. Mines stretched out in every direction, farther than the eye could see, and deeper than a religious man liked to imagine. The lakes, machinery, corroded paths, and mountains of red gravel that I'd seen through the mist last fall were spread out in the blue spring distance like Jupiter's forever. Echo was standing quietly, staring at the pit. She wore my Powr-House Blue Denim Engineer's cap, and there was red dust over her pretty white boots. I snapped her picture. She turned, smiling, and I dropped beside her. There was nothing to say; I took her hand and we backpedaled down the embankment's other side to a muddy road. There was no mist or fog, but the wind was blowing in that Hibbing way, and Echo moved closer, swinging our hands to her waist.

We walked down that road about a quarter of a mile. It was the wind and the spring and the sun, and Old Hibbing and New Hibbing were back there on the other side of the train. We walked together at the edge of everything, not caring about the mud, with the past in a gray lake at the bottom of the abyss in water that lapped the broken tracks of steam shovels and the iron that wasn't mined, wasn't harvested; but we couldn't care.

At the end of that road was the observation platform, Diamond Jubilee Days pasted all over, Hull-Rust mining company pays its respects, *But Be Careful!* . . . So I leaned out over the railing and took a picture with one hand. Then I took a picture of Echo in front of a giant shovel; and one of her in front of the observation tower; and one of her sitting on a monster tractor tire.

"Sit over there, Echo. That's right, on the tire. Go on, get right up on it, I want a picture."

She looked at me like I was crazy, or Bob; but grinned. "That's the way he was posing on the cover of the *Saturday Evening Post,* wasn't it? On a tire, wasn't he?"

"Right," I said. "No, keep my engineer's hat on; I want it propped up big."

Sunday afternoon suppers for Echo's family in Hibbing haven't changed much since she was a girl. Weather permitting, parents, in-laws, grandparents, and grandchildren gather outside Matt and Martha Helstrom's house, cut themselves sticks for roasting hot dogs, and huddle around a big outdoor fireplace. The conversation is of wild game, children, the constantly changing weather, or any great northern pike that might have been landed. At four o'clock in the afternoon the moon has risen, pale and icy in the north country sky. Matt Helstrom has killed two bears no more than thirty yards from his front door in the years he has lived outside Hibbing, and the hides are nailed skin-up on an old tractor shed out back.

I had been playing the guitar and singing for the last half hour, but it had grown too cold to continue. The session had been romantic; everyone had listened attentively, and had had comments to offer about how much I sounded like Bob—indeed, made it seem as if he were back home playing for them again. We had all sung "Blowin' in the Wind" together. Corny, I know, but not if you'd been there. Matt Helstrom, reticent at first, now seemed friendly; he had showed me his impressive collection of guns, a sportsman's tale attached to each, and now he was running movies he'd shot the previous winter, of deer feeding on hay and grass piled up on deep snow by concerned villagers. Ten or twelve deer sprang up from their feeding and raced down the service road behind Echo's house. A handheld camera followed them through the windshield of Matt Helstrom's station wagon and into a distant woods. White tails and hoofs kicking up snow through the brush. Matt Helstrom glanced at Echo and me and smiled. "He likes you," Echo whispered. "Probably 'cause you're so fair." She meant blond.

Lights came on, conversation resumed, and Echo's mother emerged from the basement with an armful of 78s. She spread them out on a sofa, and I browsed through a few—some with ECHO HELSTROM taped to the labels. Sure, Bob and Echo had listened to records together here at the Helstroms'. Probably to some of the ones I was holding in my hand. Mrs. Helstrom puts on several, well worn but playable. Spade Cooley's "Detour," Cowboy Copas's "Candy Kisses," Pee Wee King and his Golden West Cowboys, Eddie Arnold, Hank Snow . . . "That Hank Snow song there," Echo said, "'Prisoner of Love,' Bob used to sing like that, talk-singing. He'd play a couple of verses with John Bucklen, and then go into the talking. There was also some other old song he'd do that way, about a little kid who was hit by a car. It was a sad song, but you had to laugh at Bob doing it.

"He'd make up songs that way, too. Some situation would pop into his head and he'd build on it, going for the longest time. I don't think he ever wrote those songs down though; they were just fun when he'd make them up on the spur of the moment."

"Don't either you or your mother have any pictures of Bob from the old days? Snapshots, anything?"

"No, I wish I did. We never went in for that sort of thing too much. I remember once though, this fellow who was a photographer around town asked me to pose for him out in the old graveyard—where we were today! He made me put on black leotards and all that stuff. Then when we got out there, he asked me to take off my top, so he could 'shoot my back,' he said. Well, I was game enough to go out in that graveyard with him, but not game enough for that! And later when I told Bob about it, he said he didn't think he wanted me hanging 'round with that guy anymore, anyway.

"But wait, there *are* some old pictures of Bob, in my yearbook! Why didn't I think of that before? Let me look." Echo disappeared for a moment into a bedroom, returning with two dark-green *Hematites.* The first was from Bob and Echo's senior year, 1958–59. They had broken up by then, and the picture of Bob is a chubby Elvis Presley pose, with just the hint of a smirk on Bob's shiny lips. The second *Hematite* was the 1957–58 edition, Bob and Echo's eleventh-grade year, when they were still going steady. This picture is a little more like it—Bob's curly hair is mussed in a familiar fashion, his face is thinner, and a grimace of startling intensity leaps out from the page.

"Look at that face!" Echo whistled. "Boy, Bob must have *really* been mad that day."

I turned back to the first page of the yearbook, and yes, there it was . . . Bob's letter-poem, in that same shaky handwriting, blue ballpoint pen marks, fading . . .

A decrepit recording of Carson Robinson's "Ohio Prison Fire" suddenly flipped on, diverting Echo's attention. "Oh, listen to this one," she said, "this has got to be one of the earliest of those modern-type protest songs; I can't remember whether or not Bob ever heard it, but isn't it like him?" I closed Echo's *Hematite,* and tried to pay heed to the mournful tale of a prison gutted by fire—a fire that took the life of every man still locked in his cell, and apparently due to overcrowding and negligence on the part of the guards. The song could easily have appeared on Bob's album *The Times They Are A-Changin'*.

"These old records were interesting, even in those days, but mostly Bob played his own music. Not stuff he'd written, but things from the radio. He'd sit out front there on that swing and play his guitar, or perch on some old stone steps that used to lead up to our front door. He'd sit and play, alone or with John Bucklen, and I'd be the audience. The songs he'd play then weren't band songs, but quiet ones, sort of country, like what we've been listening to."

Echo was swaying slowly back and forth on Bob's old swing, dragging a foot in dirt not toyed with for some years. Another Hank Snow record scratched and clicked into action on Mrs. Helstrom's Victrola, and the simulated train sounds of muffled guitars and screaming fiddles drifted out of the yard and up toward Maple Hill.

The song ended, and Echo's mother was calling to us from a window. She'd found something special. One of Bobby's songs she'd forgotten she'd bought. Echo fumbled with the 45 spindle, dusted off the old needle, and... "Chimes of Freedom," done in Byrds-electric fashion... by a group called The Bad Omens. Mrs. Helstrom smiled her big Swedish smile and did a little bounce. Echo sat down on the daybed, slouching slightly to the rhythm. I listened and watched.

The B side was another old song. "He Was a Friend of Mine."

GUSHICON EIGHT: *Ten Thousand Dollars at the Drop of a Hat*

Frogs are singing this evening, in the marsh outside my window at Michael's Motel, a mile south of Hibbing on Highway 169. The Coleman gas furnace kicks on and off, a north country spring gale rattles the storm door to my room, and I can see dirt swirling around the top of a 250-foot high iron ore dump, only a short field away. Cars go by every five minutes or so. Very fast; and with loud, unmuffled whooshes. I have neither radio nor t.v. to break the pleasant monotony of frogs and cars. Only complimentary copies of *Argosy* and *True* magazines. "Finally the full story: How the U.S. got Che Guevera." For today's man. Today's man, field-equipped with busty broad, big cigar, bronze muscles, and everywhere-hair. But as for yesterday's . . . memories of something different. A strange collage; of marsh voices, howling wind, highway sounds . . . and distant conversations.

First paragraph of my *US* story. Richard Goldstein's deadline hovering just three days away, but what day was it now? many more words to squeeze out before Wednesday, or was it Thursday? when the piece *had* to be in the mail—my second cup of coffee sticking to the bottom of my mug, coffee the nice owner of Michael's Motel had given me, she liked me, thought it so cute I was writing about Bobby, would catch her cleaning my room and checking out the manuscript, but she fed me, every night about six that knock at my door, and she would have something hot; and in the morning about eight when I got up she would brew coffee, all I could drink,

and there were soft drinks in her icebox I could help myself to . . .
she hoped I'd be sure to send her a copy of my story.

The days like that, from eight to six working on the thing, finding it hard to put it all down straight, what was straight? taking
breaks at the Hibbing A & W rootbeer stand, eating hot dogs with
mustard and relish, drinking orangeade . . . everything was orange
there, and empty cold these long spring days; only the die-hards
stayed outside and ordered from curb service . . . driving around in
the afternoon, on the outskirts of Hibbing mostly, taking back roads,
talking to strangers in the middle of nowhere, old-timers, young
kids younger than me, or Bob, and in the evening walking with my
tray up to the motel office, stopping on the bumper of my VW to
watch the sun go down, down over the mines and the frogs and
the tall grass behind Michael's . . . and getting back to work, trying
to keep warm in front of my stove, all until ten or so when my back
hurt so much I couldn't type any longer; and it was just too hard
anyhow; I'd slip into town for some entertainment and a beer or
two. Hibbing swallowed me up like any strange city, only it was
strange in a different way now. People had begun nodding at me
in the street, and in bars; waitresses brought me the usual without
bothering to ask; and bands at both the Garden and Corner lounges
waved when I walked in. But . . . there were no interviews, I wasn't
learning anything new about Bob. I had no reason to be here.
I felt like the summer patron of some fabulous resort who has decided to stay on through the winter: An image crisis was imminent,
for relationships had changed. I was becoming part of Hibbing.

Mrs. Zimmerman was back in town, Bob's aunt had told me that
much; but Mrs. Zimmerman was never home. I called and called
and left messages but nothing. I wasn't going to give up on that,
though; if Bob Dylan's mother was in Hibbing while *I* walked the
streets, I certainly wasn't leaving until I'd at least talked to her on
the phone. And then there was the priest . . . yes! Bob Stehlin had
given me that lead. Apparently, last time Bob had been home, he
had run into one Father Hayes—from over at the Blessed Sacrament Church—and had invited him to dinner a couple of times,

talked with him about all sorts of things...I'd been over to the Blessed Sacrament Church twice looking for this fellow, but no one had been around. I mean no one. Big and stone and damp and spooky—I couldn't go back there again. Things were hidden in that church I wasn't supposed to know.

But I played my guitar a lot, all those old songs, the corny ones and the Hibbing ones, and the classic ones, and most of the others. I worked very hard in that little pine room, and slept with a host of nightmares.

GUSHICON NINE: *I Swear I See My Reflection*

It was twelve fifteen Thursday afternoon, my *US* story was finished and packaged and riding in the seat beside me . . . and I was on my way to meet Bob Dylan's mother for lunch. I was to pick her up at Feldman's, where she worked intermittently as a saleslady—she had been in Florida all winter, she'd told me that yesterday afternoon when I'd finally reached her on the phone. She'd also told me how disgusted she was with what I had written in the *Voice* . . . she hadn't seen the entire piece, just the last installment about David. Nope, he hadn't been too pleased about it either. Bob? Well . . . (Mrs. Zimmerman was furious, calling me everything a lady might in good taste) he had been reading it, following it, and had been *concerned,* she spat the word out. "Why can't you journalists stop *torturing* this boy?" she had demanded. Oh, god. I don't know, *somehow* I'd convinced her I wasn't the ogre she thought, and that I would be indebted to her for life if she would just meet me over coffee, anything! She had finally relented. *Journalist,* what a nasty ring the word had. "You're up here with that Echo, too, aren't you?" she had said. From Bob Dylan's girlfriend to his mother, in one complicated lesson. "Yes, Mrs. Zimmerman [sure, Mom], I'd love to meet you for lunch . . . [No, Mom, *honest,* I haven't done anything wrong] pick you up at work?" After she'd hung up, I'd driven way out past Chisholm, and stared at craters for the rest of the afternoon. I couldn't work; I'd wanted to tear up everything I'd written and go to church; temple; bed. (I'm good...good as my neighbor.)

But now I was trudging down Howard Street—for the last time?—and Feldman's mammoth two-story edifice loomed like some huge and inescapable witness stand. At the big glass door, a better part of valor nearly gained the upper hand...but then I was inside, smack dab in the center of the Ladies' Department, dresses and scarfs and racks and cash registers and Mrs. Zimmerman smiling and shaking my hand, more attractive than I'd imagined, and friendly as could be! She shooed away a customer and whispered that I should hurry next door to the Howard Restaurant and grab a booth, assuring me that she'd be over directly. I offered meek assent, floating back out the door in a cloud of awe at the cosmic responsibility of my task.

I had to fight for a table at the Howard—my coat and tie didn't seem to be doing much—but was ultimately successful, my prize being a large booth toward the front of the room. I waited for Mrs. Zimmerman five minutes—ten—what was I going to ask her? how could I not appear foolish? evil? Twenty minutes—why was she taking so long? was she going to bring somebody with her? a strong friend? the police? her sons? *Bob???*... I jotted furious nothings into my notebook, trying to look professional—but I didn't want that! anything but professional!... but too late, Mrs. Zimmerman had caught me, and she was standing beside the booth, slipping out of her coat.

I would be polite, gallant; I rose and helped her with her things. She smiled. I smiled. We made small talk and ordered. She didn't trust me, obviously, but there was warmth in her presence. She seemed to regret her harangue of yesterday; I told her not to, I had deserved worse. She smiled, and asked me if I was certain I wouldn't have pie for dessert. I said no, but compromised with a glass of milk. She softened.

"You know, the only two parts of your *Village Voice* story I've seen are the last, which I mentioned on the phone, and the first, which the Hibbing paper picked up from Ralph Gleason's column."

"They printed that whole first section?" I swallowed.

"No," Mrs. Zimmerman said, "I guess it couldn't have been the entire section because there was only a paragraph or so. Must have been just what Ralph Gleason quoted. But it still upset me, that business about Bob coming home for his father's funeral . . . Bob didn't want that to be printed; he didn't want his father's death written about in a national paper like that. And as for the Cadillac, he bought that for his father three years ago. That sounded awful, that he would come home and do something like buy a car at the time of his father's death."

"I suppose it did," I said, "but I certainly didn't mean it to seem that way. If you'd read the entire first section I think you would have had a different perspective on the tone. I meant that to sound nice, like, well you know, somebody who'd buy his mother a Cadillac, under *any* circumstances, would have to be a pretty nice guy."

Mrs. Zimmerman took a bite of her hamburger and looked up. Something seemed to click. "Bob Dylan is as nice and good a person as anybody in this world; he doesn't want to hurt anyone, and he hates violence; his father was the same way, you just ask anyone in this town, everybody loved him." That was true, everybody did say that. But I had just seen Bob Dylan's mother take a bite of a hamburger and leave lipstick stains on a coffee cup. It was spooky how much she resembled Bob: Under a Florida tan and a glamorous head of gray-blond hair, she was a dead ringer for him. She even had the same accent; and her eyes could belong to no one else but Bob Dylan's mother. She was extremely well dressed, too. She did have diamonds, but she wore them with taste. She reminded me of *my* mother.

"David was upset by your piece," Mrs. Zimmerman was saying, "something you had misquoted him on, or something you had said about him coming up to Hibbing and killing the principal?" That had been one of my witticisms! Were these people dense? I ignored the question and kept smiling; Mrs. Zimmerman continued.

"And as for that little girl, Echo . . . Bob took her to one or two proms, I really don't think their *affair* amounted to anything."

Hmmm. "How would you feel if someone came around snooping into your life; you wouldn't like it, would you? And Bobby's *so* sentimental.... once I took him up to Old Hibbing, when the last of the razing was being completed, and showed him where all the old buildings used to be. This was after he was grown and had left home—and he got so upset; he'd look and point and say things like 'That's where you went to *school,* Mom ... and it's gone now, isn't that *sad?*' These were *my* relics, too. You can imagine how he feels about his own past."

What could I say, except to try to change the subject? "You just mentioned something about Bob having left home ... exactly when was that? There are so many rumors."

"Bob left home at nineteen and a half, Toby, and those stories about his having run away, none of them are true. Bob never ran away, he was a normal, happy child. That's another thing, so-what if he got Cs in school? Why write that, he was just another kid when he was living here, I certainly couldn't tell anything about his being a *genius.* How can you know you have a genius in your house, when all your time is spent trying to feed him and keeping his clothes pressed?"

Oh, god. "Well, did he go straight to New York when he left Hibbing? Did he have any connections?"

Mrs. Zimmerman took a sip of her coffee and touched her napkin to the corners of her mouth. "Sure, Bob had connections in New York, but he still had to work very hard to get a start. The connections didn't hurt him any, but they certainly weren't a great deciding factor. New York was where Bob had made up his mind he wanted to go, and that was where he went. First off. He told his father, 'Let me try it; I have to see whether I can do this.' He went with our blessing. And as for losing track, or not keeping in touch ... he was in New York two days when he called back to ask if David had been shoveling the walk. He's like that, your Bob Dylan, he has always cared about his family more than himself; he would do anything. When I was in Florida, before *Nashville Skyline* had been released, he came down and sang all the new songs for me. And when I'd finally gotten a copy of the record, I called to congratulate him and to say how much I liked the Nashville sound better than any of the others, and all he said was, 'Well, Mom, maybe I can do better next time.' And, 'Do you need anything?' He's so kind, I hate to see him hurt." Mrs. Zimmerman shot me a protective smile.

"What about the name 'Dylan'—there's been much speculation as to its source? Bob took it from the poet Dylan Thomas, didn't he?"

"Of course, there was never any uncle by that name, and my maiden name is Stone. Bob changed his name for show-business reasons, and made it legal only because he had to carry two cards around to get into clubs. I remember the night he called home to ask his father about it; he said, 'Do you mind?' and his father had said, 'Bobby, of course not, what's in a name? It's the person that counts.' His father always had a great interest in Bobby's career, and would offer advice. When Bob was home once, *way* back in the folk music days, he was playing the piano like he used to—rock and roll music—and singing ... Bob's father said, 'Bobby, why don't you make a rock and roll record, and release it under another name if you're worried about your image?' Bob stopped playing and answered, 'Oh, no! I couldn't do that.' Bob's voice has always been good, he could sing like he's singing now years ago, back when he was a teenager. But no, he had to make it sound rough, that was going to be his gimmick, how he would be different. The same for the long hair, he was the first. And now look! So he's cut his off, he doesn't need that anymore, he's made it. He's forever the individual; *always* had to do it his way, and by himself. Peter, Paul, and Mary wanted him to be part of their group when all of them were first starting, but Bob wouldn't do it. It had to be his way or not at all, just as long as he didn't hurt anyone. Those so-called *vicious* stories Bob told about Hibbing and his early life, and about the rest of the family ... they never bothered anybody because Bob wrote and asked if even *that* was going to be all right. He told us he was going to make up some things, just to help him in his image, and we approved. 'How can something like that hurt us?' his father had said. We understood; Bob was the only one who has suffered from bad publicity. He wanted to sue at first—people saying that he didn't write 'Blowin' in the Wind'!—but finally he just decided, 'Well, what do I *really* care about what they say?'"

People had been eyeing us from all around the room ever since Mrs. Zimmerman had joined me at our booth, and finally it happened—we were interrupted. An older couple approached Mrs. Zimmerman, asking about Florida, and welcomed her home with big, friendly busses. I signaled our waitress for more coffee, and another couple approached; but there was no talk of Bob from any of these people. This was Mrs. Zimmerman's show. They were all very polite, lingering just long enough to say hello.

"Your friends seem glad to see you again," I said, once we were alone. "I don't suppose it's always like that in public places— I mean in other towns, where people act crazy about Bob?"

"Toby, you just don't know. This past winter in Florida, I'd go to a party or a reception or a wedding, *anything*, and sooner or later it would happen. Someone would find out I was Bob Dylan's mother, and I wouldn't have a moment's peace from there on in. People would form *receiving lines* to talk to me. Most places now, I don't even say my name is Zimmerman. And the reporters . . . they call me from all over the country, at all hours of the day and night . . . to ask the most absurd things, like the exact hour of Bob's birth! In the old days, when my husband and I lived in our house on Seventh Avenue, the kids would come . . . Bobby would say, 'You don't have to be nice to those people,' but Bob's father, he was so proud . . . he'd invite anybody in, talk with them, show them around . . ." Mrs. Zimmerman finished her coffee, but the waitress was right there to fill her cup. Mrs. Zimmerman thanked the waitress, calling her by her first name.

I wanted to get into the religious business but didn't know how to bring it up. Mrs. Zimmerman was glancing at her watch, so . . . what the hell. "I've been interested, over the years, in the repetitive use of religious symbolism in Bob's lyrics. All that seemed to come to a head with *John Wesley Harding*, written, I've supposed, at the time of his reclusion in Woodstock. This is a professional-type interview question now, I want you to be ready." Mrs. Zimmerman looked motherly and smiled. "Can you tell me anything about

Bob's religious life, the training he's had, either here in Hibbing or wherever?"

Mrs. Zimmerman kept her smile, but her motherliness took on an added brace of pride. She *was* a proud woman; that had been obvious from the start. "Toby, Bob has always been religious; in his house in Woodstock today, there's a huge Bible open on a stand in the middle of his study. Of all the books that crowd his house, *overflow* from his house, that Bible gets the most attention. He's continuously getting up and going over to refer to something. And as a child, Bob attended *all* the churches around Hibbing; he was very interested in religion, and *all* religions, by no means just his own."

"His family life in Woodstock..."

"Bob's family life and devotion to his children are very much tied in with what he's learned from religion, us his parents, and the lessons of life imposed upon him by the kind of career he's had. You wouldn't know your Bob Dylan at home...Bob Dylan with his drugs! Bob never used drugs, that was just the press again. Why, he won't even take an aspirin. His life is as regulated...Bob goes to bed every night by nine, gets up in the morning at six, and reads until ten, while his mind is still fresh. After that, the day varies; but *never* before. The kids are always around, climbing all over Bob's shoulders, and bouncing to the music...they love the music, sleep right through the piano...and Jesse has his own harmonica, follows Bob in the woods with a little pad and pencil, jots things down...these are the things Bob feels are important, Toby, and this is the way he's chosen to live his life. I mean, what's the matter with young people today is just this sort of thing, isn't it, *not* believing in the family, *not* standing up for marriage. Why, Bob could have had all the girls he wanted, for the rest of his life, if he'd chosen to do it that way. But he wanted a family—he has a beautiful one—and he believes very strongly in that institution. The violence, the assassinations, they all stem from a loss of pride in the family...don't you think so? What's wrong with young people nowadays, Toby, if it's not that?"

I shook my head and looked into Mrs. Zimmerman's eyes. I had no argument to offer.

"Bob's concert tour. . . ." But there was no stopping her.

"Probably the main reason Bob hasn't gone back out on the road is just this, the violence. He hasn't said too much about it, but I'm sure he's nervous; assassination isn't so remote a possibility for a figure of Bob's popularity. Also, I think he felt the John Lennon business, with John's wife and him nude, I think Bob felt that silly. Again, he didn't say so, but I could tell. He loves the Beatles, loved *Sgt. Pepper,* but this recent nonsense . . ."

"What about *Don't Look Back?*"

Mrs. Zimmerman's eyes narrowed. "Bob hated that movie, Toby; that wasn't Bob up there on the screen. Don't think I'm a prude or anything, because I'm not. But that movie wasn't true; it wasn't Bob Dylan."

"Do you keep up with what's written about Bob, all the stories and reviews?" Mrs. Zimmerman was checking her watch again.

"Toby, I get letters every day from people who send me articles. From all over the world. And I have a subscription to *Billboard* . . . most of the reviews this time—of *Nashville Skyline*—are better than ever before. Bob's in Nashville right now with Johnny Cash, taping a TV show . . . there are so many things happening, I can't keep them straight. Johnny is another performer whose career is finally starting to catch on fire. He and Bob are very old friends; I think John gave Bob one of his first good guitars."

Mrs. Zimmerman finished the last of her coffee and waved to our waitress for the check. "In Woodstock," I blurted, "does . . . is there ever any chance of Bob granting interviews, or even just seeing people who drop by?"

"No, not usually. Not for strangers without appointments. Like last fall, when Al Aronowitz and a photographer were setting up shots for the cover story of the *Saturday Evening Post,* I was sitting on Bob and Sara's porch holding the baby. Down at the end of the driveway I noticed two kids walking toward the house. I said, 'Bob, there are some kids coming up the driveway.' But he said it was all right, and kept posing for the photographer. He had on this big white hat, and the kids walked right up to him. One of them said, 'Hey mister, do you know if Bob Dylan lives around here someplace? Do you know him?' Bob laughed and said, 'You're talking to him,' and they almost flipped. They came up to the house and played with the baby... stayed for quite a while. But I don't think that sort of thing really happens too often; and never with a journalist."

The check came, but Mrs. Zimmerman was quick and beat me to it. "*Please,* Mrs. Zimmerman..." I protested. I wanted to pay for this one.

"No, Toby, you save your money, you've a long trip back East. Besides I asked *you* for lunch." Mrs. Zimmerman glowed motherly again and smiled in that motherly way. The check was paid, and I think I helped her into her coat. I think. We seemed to be getting along famously now. Nothing like breaking bread to heal differences. I was pleased... pleased? Shell-shocked! But did she mean those smiles?

Returning the short half-block from the Howard to Feldman's, Mrs. Zimmerman and I were stopped twice by well-wishers, and passing hellos wafted in at random. We paused at Feldman's big front door, and Mrs. Zimmerman offered her hand. "Send me a copy of your little book, now." She laughed. I promised I would; I promised and thanked her and grinned as she disappeared gracefully into the brightest, friendliest, least-assuming building in town.

Feldman's!

GUSHICON TEN: *Jack Kerouac Is Dead?*

Should I send it? There was the post office, it was open, and I was parked in an illegal zone, so I had to make up my mind. But should I? *Sure,* why not? What difference did it make at this point; and it was better than the first one, much better. But *silly* like the first, cute . . . *don't* send it, call Richard Goldstein collect and tell him you couldn't find anything more on Dylan's past worth writing about. No . . . it was silly, self-mocking even. But that was the point of all this, wasn't it? I mean, that silly things are often the most important and invariably the hardest to write about. Those childish things people do all their lives, which other people always want to hear about . . .

Send it.

The postmaster wasn't handling it like something special, even though I was mailing it Airmail Special Delivery to New York. He just took my ninety-five cents and stamped the mother up, and flipped it in a pile. Waving good-bye.

I drove straight back to Michael's Motel, didn't stop anyplace, and didn't go out of my way. I didn't drive by Bob's old house, and I didn't go by Zimmerman's. I drove up Howard Street, though— *that* was on my way—and it made me sort of sad. But that was all, I went straight back to Michael's and packed. I stuffed all my things into my Volkswagen, and left the motor running while I went into the office to pay my bill. It was only thirty-seven dollars and fifty cents for a whole week—that nice lady had fed me and talked to me and generally taken care of me for only thirty-seven dollars and fifty cents. For a week. She even waved to me from her office door as I drove off.

The afternoon was warm and nice and contented as I headed out past Echo's old house, and the radio was playing just the right kind of music. WEBC from Duluth; they were solid, top-forty format now. Smack up-to-date. Echo's house shot by. I drove on down the road a little farther and stopped the car. I had to get out and grope around in my junk for several minutes before I found it—my Powr-House Blue Denim Engineer's cap. It had gotten dirty and was crushed on one side. But I could smell Echo's perfume when I put it on. I pulled it down over my eyes and decided to make a detour. I cut back to Highway 37, heading east toward Duluth. It was only a little bit out of my way—I was going to Iowa City to rest for a few days at a friend's place, and I should have kept straight south. But I made the turn anyhow...what the shit, it's tough to always know whether you're doing the right thing. And besides, I had an itch under my belt to ride down Highway 61 one more time.

EPIGUSH

How many people were there
Who came to stare
And shake your hand
And stand beside your chair?

They used to laugh and boo and jeer
While I sat there and shed a tear
They just couldn't appreciate
But I told them 'You just wait,
Someday folks're gonna cheer!'

Now they want your autograph
Play your records on their phonograph,
And we can see who's laughing last.
You sure showed the Class of '59
You're doin' fine!

—REUNION DITTY, Echo*

* Also at this point, please cue up Rosie and the Originals' original "Angel Baby," paying special attention to verse four. I had intended to include that wonderful verse...you know, the one about Angel Baby finally coming back home oo-wah oo-wah, but couldn't get permission.

BE TRUE TO YOUR SCHOOL

Who would have believed it? I ask you in all seriousness, *who* would have believed it? *I* didn't believe it, and I'd just spent a year writing about him that way, when he was doing that sort of thing... but *I* never would have... the Hibbing High School, Class of '59, Tenth Anniversary Reunion! And *he* was there.

Saturday, August 2: Long-distance call, person-to-person from Minnesota. Oh, god...but no, it was Echo. She was breathless, this was the big weekend she'd invited me to way back in June, which of course I hadn't bothered to attend...Bob would *never*... but Echo was there in Hibbing for the festivities that evening, and class secretary Jone Hoikkala had just called to tell her...*she musn't tell a soul*...that Bob had been in touch with her from Duluth to say he was on his way, and that he would be at the reception this evening! Jone had already arranged for someone to pick Bob up— Larry Turlong, another old classmate—and she thought that *Echo* if nobody else should be told ahead of time. Now, Echo wanted *me* to fly out, charter a plane, anything! But I calmed her down and promised I'd try, and that if I didn't make it, she should call me Sunday morning, collect, to relate everything that had happened.

I tried to get a flight in time to make it out; I honestly did. The connection from Washington to Minneapolis was no problem, but from Minneapolis to Hibbing...it just couldn't be worked out. So, I waited. I waited all night Saturday without going to sleep, and then I waited most of Sunday. Finally it came, Echo's call. She was ecstatic! Bob had been there all right but hadn't gotten to the Moose Lodge, where the reception was being held, until about eleven o'clock (*the* Moose Lodge! the same place where Echo had jimmied the door for Bob at their *first meeting* twelve years ago, so he could play the piano for her). Oh, boy. She had been standing around all that time, talking to old friends—like Bill Marinac, who had been a member of Bob's first band—and glancing up at copies of my *Voice* story which were plastered all over the walls, when suddenly there he was. As simple as that. With his wife, "a delicate little thing," and "with his hair shorter than it was even in high school," and "sporting a beard." His baggy suit hung loose on his strangely thin frame. As soon as he walked in, people clustered about . . . they wanted *autographs,* here ten years later, they actually wanted autographs! . . . but Echo held back. She waited, fifteen minutes, a half an hour . . . until *finally* there was a break in the crowd. But what? . . . she couldn't go up like all the others, stupid and silly, "That's just not us," she said. She had to think up some kind of little game, "the sort of thing he'd do himself." So—she was dressed, now, in the miniest of miniskirts and the *hugest* sunglasses, that blond hair—she decided to walk up real corny and ask for his autograph, like all the others, but mocking in a nice, silly way. But . . . she got about five steps away from him, and he looked up saying, "Hey, it's you!" Then he turned to his wife and said, "This is Echo." Wow! Then he took her program and signed it, "To Echo, Yours Truly, Bob Dylan" . . . people were still jostling, there was confusion . . . but he managed to lean closer and whisper, "with his eyes great big, like old times," oh god, conspiratorial semaphores, *"I saw the story!"*

They talked for a few more minutes about nothing special . . . all those other people were still shoving, and it was hard . . . but Echo *did* get a chance to tell him about our song. She whispered, "Bob, I wrote you a song," and his eyes "got *really* big," and he said, "You *did?* What'd you call it?" And then she smiled and said, "'Boy from the North Country.'"

That was about it. After a while, the shoving got too rough for Echo, and she retreated back to another side of the room. Bob stayed about an hour, "but then some guy who had had a little too much to drink, tried to pick a fight with Bob, so he left." That was about it, Bob Dylan returning for his Tenth Anniversary Class Reunion. Who would ever have thought it?

Why, *me*, now that I think about it, *me*. *You* think about it... Makes sense, doesn't it?

Natch, it makes sense.

AFTERMOBE

Time was when metaphysics was entitled Queen of all the sciences...

—Immanuel Kant, *Critique of Pure Reason,* Preface to the First Edition

FINEST GIRLS IN THE WORLD

Oh yeah, one more thing before I let you go: Got *another* letter from Echo the other day...but return addressed "Hollywood, Calif." That's right—no use in heading out Minnesota way to see her now. The "Girl from the North Country" just ain't no more. Sad? I don't know...it really does get *awful* cold up there.

POSTGUSH

Toby Thompson puts me into U.S. Keds, clean sweatsocks, button-down fingernails, and that odd Maryland finesse, like he knows which fork to use on snails but he chooses not to use it. There's a veranda in his slang, but then a bunch of power-steer Gatorade words creep in, and just enough gutter grease to let you know he's done that too. Toby's well turned. With eternal yellow hair. And he's eager fun to be with.

So is his book. It's eager fun the way writing about rock seldom is anymore. I guess that's because most critics and essayists are too busy defending turf to realize that rock is experience music, and that the only way to transmit that kind of energy is to get out from behind your typewriter and live it. Live rock with people who hear it and create it, if possible, but more important, live it within yourself. Inner RPM is all the expertise a rock writer needs.

Pulse and balls.

That propulsion is the truest thing about this book. First, because it's hi-octane prose, open-road stuff like Mailer hitchhiking between points. But cagy the way Tom Wolfe is cagy, and so damned charming (though I can't think of a contemporary charmer). The Beat is in this writing, laid on thick over a solid base of reportage. This is a book to read while someone else is driving, just like some rock songs are only supposed to be heard in moving cars. If you don't get motion sick, you'll see what I mean about propulsion.

Propulsion and fun. Fun because this is a real story about a real writer searching out the underpinnings of a personal myth, and finding nothing but real country with real people living in it. And when you think about what that means—the land and the people in Bob Dylan's life, as Toby Thompson found them—you begin to sense that the greatest terror a rock star (or any hero) faces is the fear of being found ordinary.

Some people are going to think this book irrelevant, and others are going to put it down as an invasion of privacy. After all, Bob Dylan has a right to keep his past intact. But this book does nothing to destroy that past. It's true that there is more about young Bobby Zimmerman here than any pseudo-exclusive interview or documentary hand-job could suggest. But there's a deep respect—hell, a reverence—in Toby Thompson's approach, because the more deeply he becomes involved in discovering the hows of Bobby Zimmerman, the less he dares to pursue the whys. Hows are facts, but whys are imagination—that special bridge between a kid who called himself Dylan, and the rest of us. That bridge is Bob Dylan's only private property.

In a special sense, Toby Thompson builds that kind of bridge for himself. Despite the yearbook elegance, the one-too-many-mornings at F. Scott's grave, I think the real *meat* of this book is that you start out wanting to find Bob Dylan's "Rosebud" and you end up caring more about Toby's hidden bottle of Scotch.

Taking a biography and turning it into a postcard from home, letting the beams and girders in your work show, imposing your own private myth upon a larger public one—that's some of what New Journalism is about. And New Journalism is becoming so smug and manicured, so nipped in at the waist and square at the toes, that we can all use a lesson in how to walk around in U.S. Keds again.

I'm already looking forward to Toby Thompson's next book—the one about Chairman Mao.

—Richard Goldstein

Hey! Toby!
Where can you be?
Somebody told me
That you went back to
Washing Machine, D.C.!
How can that be?

You came to town in your Volkswagen,
And I'll tell you we sure had fun!
And now you're gone!

You played for me on your old guitar,
Took me for a ride in your little car,
Drove me near and drove me far,
We looked at the moon,
And stared at the stars,
You stood on your head in my hometown bar...
How can it be you've gone so far?

Hey? Toby? Where you are?

—TOBY'S SONG, Echo

AN INTERVIEW WITH THE AUTHOR
Terry Kelly

This interview was originally published in the Spring 2005 issue of *The Bridge,* a U.K.–based fan magazine devoted to Bob Dylan. The photographs were taken by Toby Thompson during his trips to Hibbing for the writing of *Positively Main Street.*

Toby Thompson occupies a unique place in Dylan studies. In 1971 Thompson wrote *Positively Main Street: An Unorthodox View of Bob Dylan* (published by Coward McCann and Geoghegan, Inc.). Many U.K. Dylan fans must still treasure battered copies of the paperback edition published by New English Library in February 1972. Based on a series of investigative articles Thompson had earlier written for the *Village Voice* and *US Quarterly,* the book shed fresh light on Dylan's childhood in Hibbing, Minnesota, through a series of unprecedented interviews with the singer's close family, including his mother and brother, Beatty and David Zimmerman, and his high school girlfriend, Echo Helstrom (possibly the inspiration for "Girl from the North Country"). The author of three other books as well as numerous articles for magazines such as *Vanity Fair, Esquire, Rolling Stone,* and the *New York Times,* Thompson is an associate professor of English at Penn State University, where he teaches nonfiction writing. He has been largely quiet on Dylan matters for more than thirty years, but he agreed to break his silence for this interview with *The Bridge.*

TERRY KELLY: Toby Thompson, could you say where and when you were born and tell us something about your family background and education?

TOBY THOMPSON: As *Positively Main Street* is as much a memoir as a biography, I'm happy to do this. I was born on September 15, 1944, in Washington, D.C.—then very much a sleepy Southern town—but I was conceived in New York City during wartime. So I have that dichotomy within me, one of small-town lassitude versus big-city fervor. My father was a Washington physician, but my mother had been a model in New York during the 1930s, and her brother, William Nichols, was a pioneer in 1950s television, which then was broadcast live from Manhattan. In fact, he wrote and produced *Your Hit Parade,* a weekly roundup of pop songs that were dramatized in real time. It was much a predecessor to MTV. I remember being backstage for many of these shows, and their glamour suffused me with a sense of belonging that I cherish. I still keep an apartment in New York.

During World War II, when my father was overseas, my mother house-sat a brownstone overlooking the East River, where many artists and actors congregated. My mother and uncle seemed to know everyone. As an infant, I crawled beneath the piano while Aaron Copland polished his symphonies, and when I was perhaps a year old and had not yet walked, Boris Karloff tickled my toes and said, "You shall walk." The next day I did. My uncle played boogie-woogie piano, and in later years I would stand on the radiator by his side singing "Rag Mop," an early R & B hit. That and "There's No Business Like Show Business." When I was five, the painter Max Ernst took one of my watercolors, "Girl with Sunburned Lips," and refused to give it back. All this was great fun, and after the war, moving to Washington, where my father's family lived, was a tremendous letdown. I was sent to a proper Episcopal school, St. Albans, where sons of the politically adept or socially elite studied. Senator John Kerry and Vice President Al Gore were schoolmates of mine. Gore and I were in the boarding department together.

When he lost to George Bush in 2000, I joked that it was the last opportunity I'd have to say I'd slept with a president.

Later I took a B.A. in English Literature from the University of Delaware and an M.A. from the University of Virginia, but it was St. Albans that academically shaped me.

Presumably literature and music were twin passions when you were growing up. From *Positively Main Street*, I gather that your early literary heroes included F. Scott Fitzgerald and Ernest Hemingway. (In fact, the book reveals you were a frequent visitor to Fitzgerald's grave at Rockville, Maryland, just fifteen minutes from your childhood home.) Which other "heroes"—literary and musical—shaped the adolescent Toby Thompson?

J. D. Salinger, certainly. I wrote my honors thesis at the University of Delaware about his work. It had a hipness to its language that I found beguiling, and who could not identify with Holden Caulfield? Jack Kerouac was a big influence. And later, Norman Mailer, Tom Wolfe, and that rabid band of New Journalists who ransacked American letters during the 1960s. But as an adolescent, I thought of myself primarily as a musician. I was one of those fifties kids who bought his first guitar after Elvis's "Hound Dog" topped the charts. I loved Elvis for the usual reasons and was affected deeply at his death. As, apparently, was Dylan. The Vegas-style, back-jacket photo of Bob on *Street Legal* mimics precisely that of Elvis on his last album, *Moody Blue*. A bit of our childhoods died with E. I remember being furious at my uncle for *Your Hit Parade*'s middle-of-the-road interpretations of his songs. "Make it sound like rock 'n' roll," I pleaded.

But I also was interested in jazz. Two pioneers in classical jazz guitar lived and worked in Washington: Charlie Byrd and the lesser-known but equally influential Bill Harris. Charlie Byrd was my first guitar teacher, but it was Harris who moved me. He was dark, mysterious, ethereally hip. He had been one of the Clovers, a seminal R & B group with hits like "One Mint Julep," "Love Potion Number

Nine," "Devil or Angel," and "Blue Velvet." I'd been studying classical guitar with Sophocles Papas, the principal proponent of Segovia's method in the United States and the founder of the Guitar Shop in Washington. I was bored to distraction. I begged to learn jazz, and one week Papas relented and gave me a Spanish folk song, "The Gay Ranchero." When this failed to engage me (it enraged me), he threw up his hands and said, "There's a colored man teaching here, you should try *him*." That was Harris. Papas was professorial and very old-world, but the day in 1959 when I met Harris, decked out in black continental suit, white shirt, skinny black tie, and sharp-

The author next to a Great Northern boxcar in Hibbing

toed black loafers, was like a gift from God. He was my personal introduction to hip. I'd study with him, off and on, for five years.

Harris had abandoned rock 'n' roll for solo jazz guitar, and he was much of the John Coltrane/Thelonious Monk/Wes Montgomery school. When he broke with Papas and started his own guitar studio, I would drive forty-five minutes across town to Hamlin Street Northeast for my 11:00 a.m. Saturday session, park in that all-black neighborhood, and shuffle warily toward the house. His wife would answer the door, saying, "Go down to the basement, I'll get Mr. Harris." I'd wait, and after about ten minutes, a sleepy Bill Harris would appear in immaculate white pajamas, carrying a cup of coffee, and say, "Play your lesson." He'd listen for a few minutes, head in hands, then sigh, "Give me the guitar." Off he'd go on improvisations that might last half an hour. It was the most amazing guitar music I have ever heard. He'd finish, hand back the guitar, and say, "Like that." Later, writing about Dylan, I'd realize that my fascination with black music was very much akin to his. It was part of a cultural underground that suburban or small-town white kids were just being introduced to, via radio and TV. Its hipness was our way of connecting with New York—or cities in general.

When did you first become aware of Bob Dylan? Was it a sudden or gradual "conversion" through a single song or album? Which was the first Dylan concert you attended, and how closely did you follow his career throughout the 1960s and 70s?

A harmonica player named John Kerkam introduced me to Dylan's music during the summer of 1962. I was avoiding jazz for the girls, by playing blues with Kerkam and guitarist Linn Barnes at a club called the Zen Den, in Rehoboth Beach, Delaware. Barnes and I had something of a blues act, and Kerkam sat in with us at the beach. He'd hung out in Greenwich Village, had a friend who had studied guitar with Reverend Gary Davis, and was in the know. "You ought to hear this cat, Bob Dylan," Kerkam said. "He plays blues guitar and harmonica—very interesting." Dylan's first album was out and we found a copy. I was impressed with the roughness of his blues arrangements—unusual in the wispy, white-bread atmosphere of that early folk revival. I learned most of the songs on *Bob Dylan:* "See That My Grave Is Kept Clean," "House of the Rising Sun," "Baby Let Me Follow You Down," "In My Time of Dyin'," "Fixin' to Die." The death fixation was inescapable, but it was his performance of these tunes that impressed me—the rawness of them. I didn't notice his writing until the second album, *Freewheelin'*. There it was unavoidable.

It's hard now to reconstruct the power those lyrics held. "Blowin' in the Wind," "Girl from the North Country," "Don't Think Twice, It's Alright," "Masters of War," "A Hard Rain's A-Gonna Fall." No one had written songs like those, they were brand new; hearing them was like a first reading of Tom Wolfe or Hunter S. Thompson. They seemed to emanate from our generation's unconscious. One of the first I learned was "Girl from the North Country." Eventually I would learn them all, and I began performing them, as I would intermittently in folk gigs throughout the sixties. Dylan, for me, had transmogrified from singer to writer. It was why I lionized him. His performances embodied everything I cared about: music, art, theater, and literature.

I stayed as current on his career as one could in those pre-Internet days. I did not see him in concert until 1963, at Philadelphia's Town Hall. He held that crowd in the palm of his hand, with just guitar and harmonica. Later, I remember writing a term paper on his lyrics for a modern poetry seminar, using the early *Newsweek* profile to spice it up. He seemed a mysterious older figure, a New York guy—a hipster. While the rest of us were pledging our time in gulags of the educational hinterland, Bob was getting it on with Suze Rotolo in Greenwich Village.

Prior to *Positively Main Street*, the only previous book about Dylan was *Folk-Rock: The Bob Dylan Story* (Dell Publishing, 1966) by Sy and Barbara Ribakove, which was mainly drawn from the cuttings file. Your book predated Anthony Scaduto's

biography by a year and was certainly unique in terms of its interview material. What were you doing at the time you started your research, circa 1968?

There were also Daniel Kramer's photography book and the insights provided by the film *Don't Look Back*. I'd read Bob's *Playboy* interview and Nat Hentoff's early *New Yorker* profile of him. But there was this gap in Dylanology, to use a term that did not exist. He was in seclusion in Woodstock, New York, and writers were intimidated by his disdain for the press. And by his power. In 1968 I finished graduate school at the University of Virginia and spent the summer in Charlottesville writing short stories. I'd send them off and back they'd come, with impersonally phrased rejection slips. I was desperate to get published. A friend, John Holland (later a producer for NBC's *Nightly News*) had noted my fascination with Bob and said, "Why don't you drive to his hometown, Hibbing, and see if there's a story?" So that was in my head.

And on a single day in August, Tom Wolfe published *The Electric Kool-Aid Acid Test* and *The Pump House Gang*, two books that helped define New Journalism, underscoring the notion that today's story, whatever it might be, was out there in America. You had to get out from behind your desk to find it.

I remembered that *Newsweek* article, knew Bob's family name was Zimmerman and that his father was named Abraham. So I called information in Hibbing. Abraham's number had been disconnected, but I got one for Zimmerman's Furniture and Electric and dialed. A gruff voice answered, "Zimmerman's." "Is this Mr. Zimmerman?" I asked. "I'm one of them." "Are you Abraham Zimmerman?" A pause. "Abraham passed away last June, I'm Maurice Zimmerman." I screwed up my courage and said, "Are you Bob Dylan's uncle?" He said yes, and the conversation began. I must say, the fact that Bob's father had died sparked interest. Because Bob would have been home for the funeral. I knew little of journalism but sensed I needed a news hook. I asked if anyone had ever been out there to report on Bob's life. "One fellow, years ago," Maurice said, "but

Zimmerman Furniture and Electric Company

not recently. We've always wondered why not." I summoned every bit of strength I had, and asked, "If I drove out there, would you talk to me?" "Sure, kid," Maurice grunted. "When you coming?" We made a date for the following week. I had no assignment, but my foot was in the door, and that's all you need.

Positively Main Street often reads like a picaresque novel, with yourself at the center of the knockabout narrative. The book is clearly a product of both New Journalism and a Beat-influenced approach to biography. In very general terms, what do you feel about the book now, more than thirty years later?

I like the book. It's got a smart-alecky tone that fits its time and the age of its author and protagonist, who had just turned twenty-four.

It's also cannier than it seems. It's a meta-book. I studied modern literature at Virginia and was aware of both the postmodern tradition, where experimentation rules, and that of the nineteenth-century bildungsroman, or novel of initiation—where a young hero sets out against impossible odds, acts foolishly or ineptly but confronts his enemies or the dragon, then returns home sadder, wiser. I studied Freud and I studied Robert Graves's complicated poetic theory in *The White Goddess*, which Bob mentions in *Chronicles* and which his songs would reflect in *Desire* and *Renaldo and Clara*. I knew that, in literature and psychology, one had to slay one's hero to become the hero. There was an oedipal tinge to this. To win the queen, and sleep with her, one must kill the king. All this had to do with what it meant to be a true artist. In Graves's mind, the only role of the poet was to court the muse, or moon goddess. And here we go a bit weighty. As Graves explained it, "The Theme, briefly, is the antique story... of the birth, life, death, and resurrection of the God of the Waxing Year; the central chapters concern the God's losing battle with the God of the Waning Year for love of the capricious and all-powerful Threefold Goddess, their mother, bride, and layer-out. The poet identifies himself with the God of the Waxing Year and his Muse with the Goddess; the rival is his blood-brother, his other self, his weird."

So my little book exists, however modestly, on two levels: one, the story of Toby, Echo, and Bob, and what happens realistically to them; and two, what happens metaphysically, symbolically, and psychologically to them and what they represent, both within Graves's mythic construct and within American culture. Nothing in it is fabricated; it's found.

On page 25 of the New English Library edition, you write about "the lack of any previous journalistic attention having been paid to Hibbing." In fact, the book now reads like a document from a very innocent time, before media saturation and public cynicism. Looking back, does the Hibbing of 1968–69 now feel like a different world?

It was a different world. And remains so, I've found, during my trips back. Hibbing is so far out in the middle of nowhere, so removed from the pop zeitgeist, that in 1968 it was still hard to get rock on the radio. In 1958, it was nearly impossible; Bob's father had rigged a radio wire to the house's rooftop TV antenna so Bob could pick up distant stations at night. The deep, endless forests surround Hibbing, broken intermittently by wide and primitive lakes. The town itself exists by default on the edge of one of the largest open-pit

Crippa Music

The Moose Lodge on Howard Street

iron ore mines in the world—three miles long, 458 feet deep, and a mile wide. Precariousness is in the air. You expect things to tumble any minute. The buildings are late Victorian middle-western, like a frontier town's. Quite stodgy. How Bob Dylan emerged from this environment is something of a miracle.

I'll never forget my first drive down Hibbing's main drag. I'd been on the road for three days, the windshield to my VW was smeared with bug juice, and the sun was setting at Howard Street's western end. I'd found an FM station from Duluth, sixty-odd miles east, and as I turned down Howard Street, Bob's voice exploded from my speakers. It was "Just Like a Woman." If that station playing that song at that moment wasn't a sign, I couldn't recognize one.

Craning my neck, I edged past buildings where Dylan had spent his youth: the Androy Hotel, Crippa's music store, the L&B Café, Collier's B-B-Q, the Moose Lodge, Sammy's Pizza, and all those kick-ass miners' saloons, as he sang, "When we meet again, introduced as friends, please don't let on that you knew me when, I was hungry and it was your world." Hairs stand on my neck today as I remember it. I drove all the way out Howard Street to where its macadam dropped jagged chunks into that vast expanse of mine. Then I turned back toward the Androy and booked a room.

This was the height of the counterculture era, and my Levis, wool turtleneck, and leather jacket should not have turned heads. But when I walked into the hotel bar, everybody stared. It was a piano bar, and customers gathered about it singing songs like "Tiny Bubbles." I had one beer, then moved down Howard Street to the Kahler motel. Same scene. I sat at the bar next to a fortyish guy with graying hair and ordered a drink. He asked me where I was from. I told him and said I was here writing about Bob Dylan's boyhood. Did he know him? "Yeah," the guy said. "I used to be his babysitter."

It went like that for days. Bob had only moved from Minnesota to New York in January 1961. So everyone remembered him. Shopkeepers, former teachers, his high school principal, the young couple who had bought his mother's house. I walked the streets and talked to everyone. It was a bit like Bob's pursuit of Woody Guthrie. I sat in his boyhood room on the edge of his bed and imagined Gene Vincent records spinning on his Victrola. I saw where he had broken the brass pedal of a piano at the 1958 Jacket Jamboree talent contest in his high school auditorium, as he pounded the keyboard screaming Little Richard songs. I sat in his seat in his music and English classrooms. I *lived* at the Androy, where Bob had his bar mitzvah celebration. I remember thinking that reporting was the most exciting thing I had ever done and that I'd always do it. I was not yet wise to its pitfalls.

Echo Helstrom comes across in the book as an open-hearted free spirit, willing to share virtually all of her memories of Dylan with you, in a very uncensored fashion. You capture her in a

very sympathetic and even fond manner, giving every impression of falling for her charms. What was her reaction to the way she was portrayed in the book, and did contact with the alleged "Girl from the North Country" end with the publication of *Positively Main Street*?

Echo *is* a free spirit, and her open-heartedness became the center of my book. Nowadays, she's something of a folk heroine, featured in most biographies, in the current Seattle/Dylan show [the exhibition "Bob Dylan's American Journey, 1956–1966," which originated in Seattle at Experience Music Project and later traveled to

Echo Helstrom in Hibbing

Echo in front of the boarded-up Hibbing Hotel

the Weisman Art Museum in Minneapolis; see the "Preface to the New Edition" in this book], and even as the inspiration for a Portland, Oregon, rock group called Echo Helstrom. But I was the first to write of her. And I did not find her immediately. Somebody said, "You ought to contact this girl Bobby dated in high school," but I was near the end of that first trip to the north country (to Minnesotans, that region hard by the Canadian border, hours north of Minneapolis) and was hesitant. I thought I had too much material as it was. But I called Echo's home and spoke to her mother, who was very nice and who said she'd relay the message to Echo in Minneapolis, where she lived. I was leaving next morning, and

I believe Echo called back that night. She said she'd speak with me next evening. I also had an appointment in Minneapolis with David Zimmerman, Bob's brother. Their mother, Beatty Zimmerman, had been away, and I had not been able to interview her that trip. So I caught Echo nearly by chance.

She was striking in appearance. She had Scandinavian blonde hair, looked vaguely like Brigitte Bardot, was surprisingly friendly but tough. I remember Tom Jones was on the record player in her apartment as I interviewed her. She wore high black boots with a houndstooth-check suit, its skirt fashionably abbreviated. We chatted that night for perhaps three hours, and I realized immediately she knew Bob better than anyone out there—that they had been soulmates. In *Chronicles,* he calls her his Becky Thatcher. They were wholly American kids who shared dreams of a wider world, and I wonder if his development as a romantic and his eventual escape from Hibbing would have been so rapid without Echo's support. They were both outsiders—he a Jew in a town rife with prejudice, and she a poor girl from the wrong side of the tracks—but they believed in each other.

To answer your question more directly, we *have* stayed in touch, she continues to report that my book about Bob is her favorite, and yes, I did fall for her charms. The following spring, on my second trip to Hibbing, we had a tiny romance. It's dramatized in *Positively Main Street.* The romance was delightful, but psychologically complicated for both of us.

Before that happened, I returned home to Washington and wrote up what I'd learned on my first adventure. I decided to use myself as a character, because in a way I was the archetypal Dylan fan. Quite narcissistic, in the Christopher Lasch sense of needing someone grander to complete one's psyche. I was fanatical about Dylan, as was much of my generation. So why not use that? I composed the piece chronologically, starting with my encountering Bob's babysitter, and taking it through sixty pages of narrative until my finale with Echo in Minneapolis. I had no assignment and had no real idea what to do with the story. I pitched it via telegram to *Esquire* and *Harper's,* but they weren't interested. New York's *Village Voice,* then, was the counterculture's mouthpiece, *Rolling Stone* being still a San Francisco upstart. So I sent it, blind, to them. I waited perhaps a month, then telephoned Diane Fisher, the editor I had mailed it to. She said, "I was just about to contact you. Your piece is awfully long." Yes, I know, go ahead and reject it. "How would you feel if we serialized it in six consecutive issues?" How would I feel? Fabulous is what, with six times the exposure and six times the money. She cut it slightly, and the first excerpt was published in March of '69, way back on page 75 or something. It was slugged "Bob Dylan's Babysitter!" Other newspapers immediately began writing about it. The chapter got so much attention that the following week's moved up to about page 10, edging closer to page 1 until the last chapter with its banner headline, "Dylan's Girl from the North Country," with my name below, actually made it. I received twelve book offers, got an agent, and was off.

Richard Goldstein, who wrote for the *Voice* and had essentially invented rock journalism in 1966 with his Pop Eye column, had been hired as editor of a counterculture journal called *US,* which would be published as a Bantam paperback, along the lines of *The New American Review.* He telephoned me and said, "I don't know where you've been, but you've arrived." He asked whether I had held back any material from the *Voice* series, and whether I'd be willing to drive back out to Hibbing for a second trip. I called Echo and asked if she would accompany me to Hibbing, to show me some of the spots where she and Bob hung out, and she agreed. So I was back on the American road.

I picked her up in Minneapolis on a Friday afternoon, and she looked fabulous in a gray Austrian cape with a short skirt and knee-high white boots, very mod sixties-ish. We drove north on what then was the rural two-lane to Hibbing, talking like we'd known each other forever. I had a half pint of Scotch in my glove compartment, and after a while I offered her a drink. She accepted. We shared that half pint and got to Hibbing around ten o'clock, just as the miners' saloons were rocking. There were four or five of them, and each featured an accordion-driven polka band. In *Chronicles,* Bob writes about hearing those bands as a kid, and I've always thought his affinity for the harmonica came from listening to those accordions wheeze. Very Lawrence Welk midwestern. Anyhow, we danced, talked, drank Grain Belt Premium beer, and closed the bars. At some point I stood on my head, and my change, wallet, and car keys spilled onto the dance floor. She laughed and we knew a connection had been made.

For the next couple of days we were inseparable. She took me everywhere that she and Bob had hung out, to the pizza parlors and teen canteens, to the Moose Lodge, where she had jimmied the door with her penknife and he played piano for her the first night they connected, to old Hibbing, its abandoned buildings and the red dust mines, and to meet her family. Her house was in the country, on a service road paralleling the woods. I listened to the '78s her mother had kept—the same ones he wrote about in *Chronicles*—the Hank Williams and Jimmy Rodgers cuts that had been his earliest exposure to that music. Echo's father, a tough workingman and hunter, had bear skins nailed to his tractor shed, and the old house where he and Mrs. Helstrom lived still had an outhouse. They enjoyed me, particularly the father. "He likes you 'cause you're fair," Echo said. Meaning blond. They held a Sunday cookout for me and I played and sang a lot of Bob's songs. Including "Girl from the North Country." It was confusing for them, I think. My theatricality and boyish enthusiasm made them feel as if Bob had come home, in some way. To use Graves's terminology, I seemed Bob's "blood-brother, his other self, his weird." Everybody's feelings on that were decidedly mixed.

Echo and I finished the weekend by visiting Hibbing's radio station, where Echo sang a song she'd written, called "Boy from the North Country," to my guitar accompaniment. I have a tape of that. The DJ, a bored young guy on the day shift, interviewed us enthusiastically for hours. I sang and played guitar, and the switchboard lit up like neon. Hey, it was the sixties. But we said our adieus that afternoon. I needed to finish researching and write my *US* piece, so I stayed on in Hibbing. She rode back to Minneapolis with a friend.

That week I made an all-out assault on Beatty Zimmerman, trying everything I could to land an interview. At first she dodged my calls, but eventually I reached her at work. "You're up here with that Echo!" she said. But she agreed to meet me for lunch.

The interview with Dylan's mother in Howard's Restaurant is arguably the highlight of the book. (Since she mentions Dylan was then in Nashville, for a recording of the *Johnny Cash Show* at the Ryman Auditorium, we can presumably pinpoint your interview as on or around May 1, 1969.) Considering how displeased Mrs. Zimmerman had been about your initial *Village Voice* article, she comes across as very open and accommodating. The specificity of the details she provides is wonderful: Dylan phoning home after reaching New York for the first time to ask if David "had been shoveling the walk"; Dylan traveling down to Florida to play his mother his new songs for *Nashville Skyline;* or the much-repeated story of Dylan's Bible stand in Woodstock. Did you feel a whole new Bob Dylan was revealed by his proudly defensive mother?

She didn't reveal a new Bob Dylan so much as confirm impressions I had received in Hibbing of the old one. I've interviewed a lot of people since Mrs. Zimmerman, but I don't think I've been more nervous than sitting down with her. Which I did on May 7, 1969. At first she was defensive and accusatory, chiding me for upsetting David and for getting details wrong about the Cadillac Bob had bought for his father. "Why can't you journalists stop torturing this boy!" She told me that Abraham had been sick for twenty-five years, and that publicity had helped kill him. But within minutes she became motherly and protective—of me! "Eat your dessert," and the like. I realized I was in the presence of a true Jewish mom, one that clearly had shaped Bob's character. With curly blonde hair and blue eyes, she was his spitting image. She had a first-family-of-the-town glamour. Her side of the family owned Hibbing's movie theaters, and she was quite theatrical. She gave me wonderful quotes, and if I'm not mistaken I was the last serious journalist to interview her. I wish I could reproduce our entire session here. Robert Shelton had gotten to her first, but his book would remain stalled for many years.

I thanked her, then holed up to write my piece. In a few days I mailed it off, then drove back to Minneapolis to see Echo. We spent one last evening together and it was very sad. It was as if Bob, or someone vaguely comparable, had reentered her life and now was leaving. The emotions I felt were too complicated to name. The next morning, I headed back to Washington.

Later I realized that, despite journalistic proscriptions against such behavior, our romance fit the bildungsroman format I had in mind for *Positively Main Street*. And indeed the mythic one. Her name was Echo Star Helstrom, for God's sake, "sister of mirage and echo," as Graves writes, with "hair curled honey-colored to white hips," and more than one Narcissus might love her.

That summer I wrote my book, realizing I had this construct. Somewhere in there she sent me "Toby's Song." I was touched. Personally, and because Echo was Bob's north country muse, having inspired one of his most endearing songs. I'd come out of the East a nothing writer, testing the winds of adventure, found success, courted the muse, slain my hero's calculated mythology by revealing his relative normality, "become" my hero, then retreated home. Sadder and wiser, I'm afraid, for knowledge has its price. Nothing is free, and the wicked messenger is universally despised.

Did Echo relate stories about Dylan that you chose not to use in *Positively Main Street* for legal, personal, or other reasons? Are there any untold Dylan stories from your Hibbing research that you could safely reveal now?

The only thing she asked me not to publish was what he wrote about her in her high school yearbook. She thought it too personal. But the captivating thing about Bob's early prose is that it reads just like later Dylan—the dropped consonants at the end of words, the faux slang, the poetry of it. His yearbook comment comically depicts an incident he mentions in *Chronicles,* concerning Echo's

Echo leaning against the wall of Escape-a-Go-Go, a coffee shop in Hibbing opened by David Zimmerman

father running him off one night with a shotgun and "his flashlight on my ass." Funny, rambling, "Bob Dylan's 219th Dream," so to speak. But it ends with him writing, "Love to the most beautiful girl in school." I also didn't get into details of their intimate life, which as teenagers' was typically clandestine and hurried. She probably was his first lover.

Her stories about Bob continued after my book was published. He telephoned her after he'd read it, and said, "You came off pretty good in the book." He calls every few years or so. My name has a way of coming up. Echo moves a lot, but he has this uncanny ability to find her.

Another very accommodating interviewee was Angel Marolt, the young Hibbing housewife who shows you round Dylan's childhood home at 2425 East Seventh Avenue in Hibbing, even giving you a tour of the former bedroom of the young Bobby and David Zimmerman. Again, you handle the scene very sensitively, but do you now find that kind of journalistic approach intrusive? In fact, the book contains a sort of stoned soliloquy on the very same question, when you seem to question whether you are "violating [Dylan's] past."

If violating someone's past is reporting accurately on it, then I'm guilty. But I hold with Tom Wolfe's dictum in his *New Journalism* text that "A writer needs at least enough ego to believe that what he is doing as a writer is as important as what anyone he is writing about is doing and that therefore he shouldn't compromise his own work. If he doesn't believe that his own writing is one of the most important activities going on in contemporary civilization, then he ought to move on to something else he thinks is . . ." Bob wrote in *Chronicles* that "as for the press, I figured you lied to it." He'd spun wild yarns about his past, yet I discovered that he had enjoyed a fairly typical midwestern childhood that made his evolution from it more fantastic than if he'd run away to a carnival, lived in Gallup, New Mexico, or never known his parents. In fact, he had called his parents to ask them if they *minded* his telling these lies. He was like us, yet he'd *become* Bob Dylan. How strange is that. I believe we need to know all we can about our cultural icons, particularly those who influence us directly. As for intrusiveness, forget it. We need to know what shaped our heroes, where they're coming from and what their agendas are. This view has grown more acceptable regarding political figures' lives, but less so with artists'.

Regarding the Marolts' purchase of Mrs. Zimmerman's house, the oddest codicil to that arrangement is the one Bob insisted upon: that he perpetually be allowed to visit. On a recent trip to Hibbing, a neighbor told me that Bob still occasionally will call to ask if he might stop by. A car will arrive, a dark figure will emerge and disappear into the house, where it will sit in its old bedroom for half an hour, summoning spirits.

A practical question: Did you use a tape recorder or a pen and shorthand notebook during your time in Hibbing? Much of the recalled dialogue was presumably transcribed *after* the event. Does this mean there is a fictive element to the reportage about Hibbing? (I'm thinking about the way Echo Helstrom picks you up for embroidering a story about the young Dylan serenading her family with a Bobby Freeman hit song?)

I took detailed notes as I was interviewing my subjects, and filled in gaps quickly thereafter by writing everything I could remember about the conversations, physical details, and moods. I did not use a tape recorder, but (as is often the case with highly interesting material) found I had nearly a photographic memory for quotes. At some point I sent Echo the transcript of her remarks, and she reviewed them for accuracy. That's where I think she caught the Bobby Freeman mistake. For some reason I'd remembered the story as their having had a fight, she refusing to speak to him, and his going to her house with guitar in hand, then serenading her with "Do You Want to Dance?" until she relented. In fact, as I recall, he'd merely phoned her to play the song, saying he was on the recording. It was such a funny mistake I included it in the book.

There is no fiction in *Positively Main Street*. The finds were fantastic enough.

David Zimmerman was clearly suspicious of your motives and was reportedly unhappy with the way he was quoted in your

articles in the *Village Voice*. But some of his offhand comments about his famous brother are pure gold. (I'm thinking particularly about the way you quote him, when he blithely plays down Dylan's almost iconic 1966 motorcycle accident: "He was riding around the backyard on the *grass* and slipped. That's all.") Do you believe such fascinating insights alone make the book's approach worthwhile?

As I've already stated, the book's approach was aesthetically calculated. But David Zimmerman, as the younger brother of the hippest pop figure extant, was in an impossible position. He was generous to have seen me (could he not have phoned for Bob's okay?), but he did take a defensive attitude and was trying a bit hard to come off cool. It didn't work. I wrote the scene as it happened, and I'm sorry if it caused him discomfort. But I felt I needed to portray him as accurately as I could. The motorcycle wipeout no doubt injured Bob, but primarily it was his excuse to quit the rat race, as he admits in *Chronicles,* and to terminate a lifestyle that had become intolerable. He was killing himself with exhaustion, and possibly with drugs. In his 1969 *Rolling Stone* interview, he said as much: "I was on drugs, a lot of things. A lot of things just to keep going, you know?" John Lennon, in *Lennon Remembers,* confirms this: about the *Eat the Document* tour of 1966 in England, he says, "I just remember we were both in shades and both on fucking junk." To see Dylan in that movie is to see someone very near death.

At one point, Echo reveals that journalist Robert Shelton had interviewed her first, in May 1968, several months before you reached Hibbing. Dylan had clearly supplied Shelton with Echo's name and details, suggesting his old friend's book was virtually "authorized." Although Shelton's Dylan biography would eventually be long delayed—not appearing (ironically enough, from New English Library) until 1986—was there any sense of professional rivalry on your part, as though you were involved in a journalistic or publishing "race" with Shelton to get *your* Dylan book out first?

To me, at age twenty-four, Shelton was the old guard, a *New York Times* reporter who had "discovered" Dylan, and who had come to Minnesota laden with greenbacks to pay sources, and who already had a contract. There was pressure to "beat" him, journalistically, but my *Village Voice* stories had already done that. After they appeared, he wrote me a snippy note saying that I'd quoted him inadvertently from one of Bob's liner notes, and not to do so in the future. I wrote him back to say that he could quote me any time he wished. Having mentioned that, Shelton's biography is probably the most valuable one we have. He was Dylan's friend and he had Dylan's complete cooperation. He has more extensive interviews with him than any other writer. He shies away from the drug issue, though. As does Dylan, in *Chronicles, Volume One.* Perhaps he'll get to it.

I think some of the strongest elements in *Positively Main Street* are the local detail extracted from Hibbing, such as the descriptions of Crippa's record store, where only *John Wesley Harding* and *Dylan's Greatest Hits* are in stock and where the saleslady who had sold Bobby Zimmerman his first harmonica uttered the classic critical comment: "Bob doesn't sell too well in Hibbing. People don't like his voice." Apart from the interview material, did you aim to capture the essence of Dylan's childhood home in stray, but telling, images?

Absolutely. The impressionistic tone of the book's descriptions were meant to do that. I wanted the reader to feel he was walking Howard Street with me. And experiencing the excitement I did.

In his *Rolling Stone* interview with Jann Wenner (November 29, 1969), Dylan expressed his displeasure at your *Village Voice* articles about Hibbing. But he seemed mainly concerned about references to his lately deceased father rather than the articles per se, even calling the pieces "accurate." What did you feel about being publicly rebuked by Bob Dylan (some fans may take

The front window of Crippa Music, with Echo

it as a great honor!)? Did you have any regrets and did you have any additional feedback from Dylan or his office regarding the articles or later *Positively Main Street*?

Frankly, the pieces had received so much attention, Bob's reaction did not surprise me. And I thought his comments prescient. His father had just died, theirs had been a difficult relationship, and he felt protective of his memory. He chastised me for "making fun" of some good people in Hibbing, and I *had* been snotty in a way— certainly in that early *Voice* series. But I was making fun the way the counterculture made fun of squareness, not realizing at first the seriousness of these people's lives. Mentors of Bob's, like B. J. Rolfzen, his high school English teacher, and Val Peterson, his music teacher, helped shape him. They were enormously proud of him. Wenner prodded him to say something negative about my series; he seemed irritated that the *Voice* had scooped him. But when Bob said I had some lessons to learn, he was right. I began to learn them during that second trip to Minnesota, and the process of "becoming" that my character endured, in *Positively Main Street,* embraced the learning of those lessons.

A. J. Weberman mentioned you in his Dylan "interview" published in the *East Village Other* in January 1971, claiming he knew you and that you were interviewing various old friends of the singer. What did you make of Weberman, the Dylan Liberation Front, and "Garbology"?

I didn't meet A. J. Weberman until 1974. Wenner introduced us. A. J.'s comment was "Are you *the* Toby Thompson?" I saw A. J. less as a reporter than as a performance artist. The tricksters were out-trickstering Bob. And they were driving him crazy. But there was a period there, in the late sixties, when he lost his sense of humor. The Dylan Liberation Front seemed wacky, but it may have had its point about Bob (during one period of his life) having been enslaved to drugs. Except that the late sixties, according to his mother, were years when he wouldn't even take an aspirin.

Toby, apart from your brief foreword to Dave Engel's *Just Like Bob Zimmerman's Blues: Dylan in Minnesota* (Amherst Press, 1997), I have seen nothing more of your writing about Dylan since *Positively Main Street.* Did you intend to write more about Dylan? Is there an unpublished follow-up to *Positively Main Street* hidden away somewhere?

I wrote of Dylan briefly in my third book, *The Sixties Report,* regarding that book's thesis, which was the white middle class's co-option of hip. And I reviewed *Blood on the Tracks* for the *Wash-*

ington Post. But the closest I've come to writing at length about Dylan was in 1994, when I had an assignment from *Rolling Stone* to profile him. The situation came about like this: I was digging through boxes of research material from *Positively Main Street* when I came across a letter Wenner had written me after the publication of my *Voice* series. It complimented me on my work and suggested that if I ever had anything like it again to let *Rolling Stone* know, as they paid well. I thought it an amusing piece of nostalgia, so I Xeroxed it and mailed the copy to Jann with a note saying, "How could we have grown so old?" I asked whether he'd ever thought of doing a full profile of Bob, not just a Q & A. He called me the next afternoon. "Do you have access?" he said. No, but given the circumstances of *Positively Main Street,* I thought Bob might talk to me. "I'll phone his publicist," Jann said. That call was the first of numerous, over the next few months, between Bob's Bel Air publicist, Elliot Mintz (later to represent Paris Hilton), myself, and Wenner. If you think Bob's hard to reach, try Elliot Mintz. This was before cell phones were common. I'd call about ten, Pacific Coast Time, and his service would answer, saying, "This is Elliot, I'm not here, but try the car phone." I'd try that number and another service would answer, saying, "You've reached my car phone, I'm not here, but please try the house." I'd try that number and a service would answer, saying, "This is Elliot, you've reached the house, please try my phone by the pool." I'd call there, and the round robin would recommence. I finally did, of course, reach Elliot. He was quite friendly. I explained that for this assignment I would not be satisfied with just a question-and-answer format, but that I required profile access—that time-intensive, hanging-out quotient that requires visits not only with one's subject at home but interviews with his family, friends, colleagues, etc. Elliot said he understood, but that as he received interview requests daily, why didn't I write Bob a letter expressing my thoughts? I was happy to do this. You'll recall that Bob had not cooperated on even a modest profile since Nat Hentoff's *New Yorker* one, in 1965. To get such cooperation would be a journalistic coup. His career seemed at a nadir. He had released two back-to-back folk albums of songs he hadn't written, *Good As I Been to You* and *World Gone Wrong,* and I sensed that, even though critics hinted he was washed up, he might be heading in a new direction. So I sat down to compose a letter that I hoped would win his confidence, inform him of my activities since *Positively Main Street,* provide a kind of curriculum vitae, mention a few mutual friends, and hint at the lessons I'd learned.

This is what I wrote:

Dear Bob,

I was listening to *World Gone Wrong* recently and got thinking about traditional blues and English ballads, even remembering my first hearing Mississippi John at a coffee house in Washington, two weeks after the Spottswoods brought him up from Avalon, and how he'd play Candy Man or somesuch and when people applauded he'd play it again sheepishly thinking that's what they wanted, and when they applauded twice he'd pull his hat lower and play the song another time . . . then hearing Pat Webb do Snakes in My Backyard, his detailed, aggressive picking . . . then Dave Van Ronk doing Grizzly Bear, and remembering Sonny Terry dying alone in Queens, and Lightnin' whom I never met singing Better Move Your Baby, him dead too.

So I found myself excavating stuff from my first trip to Hibbing in 1968, which included a letter from Jann Wenner after my *Voice* series appeared, saying "If you ever have anything like it give us first shot," and my jotting him a note last month asking how did we get so old and suggesting an update on you, still young at fifty-three and much alive. He concurred, so that's what this letter's about.

Many roads since *Positively Main Street,* my little book about Hibbing. A young book, my God, embarrassingly so, but written with youthful energy and crammed with all the arrogance and longing an adolescent can muster. I did make fun, as you noted of my *Voice* series, but I hope that kidding was mitigated in the book by my true affection and respect for the north country. If *Positively Main Street* has any value, I suppose, it's with my intuition that the star's and fan's predicaments are similar, that they're metaphorically the same person . . . that even in rock, the hero and his supplicant, the rival and his weird, are "blood-brothers" or "other selves" as Robert

Graves put it, and that by becoming (lite*rar*ily) Bob Dylan in the book's final sections I'd squared that circle. In a real sense I did become you in Hibbing, and was treated as you might have been as a teenager. I'll never forget your mother urging me to eat dessert at the Howard, or Echo vamping outside Crippa's and the L&B.

Let me jot a few liner notes: After *Positively Main Street,* I spent four years on the road searching for the Great American Bar. Needed a drink. *Saloon* emerged from that trip, a book conceived the night before George Wallace was shot in Laurel, Maryland. I had spotted Arthur Bremer at a place called the Varsity Grill. Even amid that bar's strangeness—motorcycles ripping through the discotheque, rental police macing patrons, coeds slathering walls of the Ladies *Stick Pigs* with their own blood—Arthur Bremer stood out. I recognized him immediately the next day and sensed that, barwise, it was time to move along. I cased Iowa, Illinois, the entire length of the Mississippi River, both banks, the Northern Rockies, and every state in the continental U.S. searching for a saloon where, if nothing else, the center would hold. I found the best in Montana, Missouri, Wisconsin, and Iowa. Places where people stood before carved front-and-back-bar sets, as if they were altar pieces in renaissance cathedrals, and talked about America. I found a saloon in Butte called Luigi's, which featured hundreds of mechanical insects, wired to Luigi's feet and hands, that danced to his one man band. I found a bar in Chicago called The Midget's Club, run by an ex-Singers Midget named Parnell St. Aubin, who'd been a Munchkin in *The Wizard of Oz,* and who kept his saloon midget-size with three-foot-high bar and tiny stools that supported construction workers who sat with knees around their ears cradling short bottles of Bud. "If I depended on the midget trade," Parnell told me, "I'd starve." I found saloons in Idaho ghost towns where all ten residents gathered each evening to drink, and where it took visitors hours to drive the twenty miles of bad road in....

Then a book about the sixties that examined our intrigue with hipsterism (White Negro redux) tracking various adherents, among whom were an ex–New Orleans hooker, a professional drag racer (speed freak), an Apollo astronaut (Michael Collins, speed freak), an ex–Green Beret, a female Viet vet, an ex-Hefner bunny and strangest of all, the pro-footballer Joe Don Looney, who'd become Swami Muktananda's elephant boy in Ganeshpuri.

In 1976 I began spending summers in Livingston, Montana, at the 1899 Murray Hotel, where your pal Sam Peckinpah spent his final years shooting holes in the ceiling and otherwise delighting locals. By this time (1979–84) Sam was a recluse. Months passed when he wouldn't leave his apartment. There was a high-stakes poker game in the Murray bar, and I remember one afternoon he appeared there after a six-week hiatus, placed a thousand dollars on the table, quickly lost seven hundred, took the remaining three, said "Boys you'll never get this," and ate it. Warren Oates was around then, as were Brautigan, Buffett, McGuane, Margot Kidder, Russell Chatham, Jim Harrison, Peter Fonda, Jeff Bridges and others who in a sense were opting out. We built something in Livingston and it's lasted . . .

Drifting, I wrote a book about the Manhattan office of the FBI and its investigations of organized crime during the 1980s—not a departure for me thematically, since its hero was an agent who'd been a rock lyricist and, within the bureau, sublimated his longing to be a novelist and actor by creating elaborate undercover scenarios in which his character starred. Currently I'm writing a novel about a teenage rocker (aka Rick Nelson) who's lured home to TV as an adult when his stepfather (aka Gleason/Kovacks/Allen) enlists his efforts for a comeback. Ending, naturally, with somebody's murder.

I've written many profiles—of Norman Mailer, Gleason, McGuane, Gary Snyder, Tom Wolfe, Hunter Thompson, David Lynch, Dolly Parton, Raquel Welch, Tom Brokaw, etc.—and have a steady gig teaching nonfiction writing at Penn State, where the kids stay intrigued by your music and pump me for what little I know of your life. . . .

My task, in a *Rolling Stone* profile, would be to convince them (and those faithful who've bought the mag since the late sixties) that in many ways your music is better than ever, that it's ageless, and to give everyone a sense of where you are in your life. I'd hope to convey, as one of my favorite painters, Robert Henri, suggested in his book *The Art Spirit,* "An interest in the subject; something you want to say definitely *about* the subject." This being, "the first condition of a portrait."

That's what I'd like a shot at, to paint your portrait in words. It surprises me that people are readier to pose for a photographer than for an author, when the camera can be far more revealing (Avedon's drifters, his portraits of Oscar Levant, Kramer's of you) than the pen. A profile is a *take,* and so long as one gets the facts right, who cares about the author's vision? Fiction, poetry, drama, nonfiction . . . we end up writing about ourselves anyway, or some facet thereof.

It would be a kick to sketch you. To do an interview, hang out, take a walk, see a movie, *make* a movie, play a tune, meditate, micturate, whatever. If you're not up to it, no sweat. But we might make something good.

Toby

A few days later, Elliot called to say that he'd given Bob my letter, and that he'd be having dinner with him the following week to discuss the matter. He also suggested that I send a fresh copy of my book, as it had been so long since it was published. What do you write for an inscription to Bob Dylan in your book about him? I wrote, "To Bob. Thanks for the music." I called Elliot that next week. He said he had met with Bob, and that "he'd been extremely moved by your letter." He also appreciated receiving the book. But he felt that he just didn't have anything new to say. I assured Elliot that Bob's remarks were secondary to his participation in being profiled, and that whatever he had to say would be acceptable. I also mentioned that I had been working with editors at the *New Yorker,* and that if *Rolling Stone* didn't pan out for some reason, the *New Yorker* might. Elliot said he'd get back to me, and he did, to report that Bob wasn't saying yes and he wasn't saying no, but felt he needed to ruminate on his decision. These conversations continued throughout the summer, with Bob either unwilling to make up his mind or uneasy with the commitment. Eventually I stopped calling. I'm still waiting for a green light from Elliot, but my hopes aren't high.

What did you think of Dylan's *Chronicles*?

It's first rate. I teach memoir writing at Penn State and am familiar with contemporary examples of the form. Bob's a hip enough reader to know that memoir owns the experimental juice, that form and structure are important in memoir but that voice is everything. His voice in *Chronicles* is consistently powerful, but malleable with the intentional time shifts. Up front, it's his voice at age twenty, then it's his at twenty-eight or thirty, next it's his at age forty-six. Then it finishes back at age twenty-one or twenty-two. The voice is intense and nearly audible. A friend remarked, listening to Sean Penn's audio version, "I feel like I'm inside Bob Dylan's head." I admire its structure, too. It's like a song's. The time shifts make for at least one bridge, and it seems to ape what he describes as the triplet approach to singing or songwriting.

I also appreciate its modest length. How wise he was neither to tackle his entire life in one volume, nor to concentrate just on the early years. The whole life would have been intimidating, the early years of interest only to folkies or Dylan freaks like us. Its length and structure contribute mightily to its long ride on the *New York Times* best-seller list. He didn't need another double album. *Self Portrait* was enough.

It's clear, also, that he is one of our more adept critics. His assessments of the work of Robert Johnson, Roy Orbison, Ricky Nelson, Dave Van Ronk, Harry Belafonte, Johnny Rivers, Len Chandler, and other figures are remarkable. He began this brand of criticism with the much-maligned liner notes to *World Gone Wrong*. He also, in *Chronicles,* is a first-rate sketch artist. The brief portraits of David Crosby, Tiny Tim, Gorgeous George, Izzy Young, Fred Neil, Albert Grossman, Suze Rotolo, Bobby Vee, John Hammond, Sun Pie, and the publishing exec Lou Levy are priceless.

But the longer portraits of Ray Gooch and Chloe Kiel are complex and layered with mystery. Why haven't we met them before? Correct me if I'm wrong, but their names appear in no biography of Bob. Could they be projections of his own divided psyche... Ray, the competent man of the world, the toolsmith, the gun collector, the would-be warrior, and Chloe, the dreamy, slightly stoned, performance-oriented homebody? Bob's not certain whether they are siblings or lovers. I'm not certain they are real. Chloe was the heroine of Longus's second-century novel *Daphnis and Chloe.* She was an orphan, nurtured by sheep, and is described as "a naive lily-white girl" who falls for the youth, Daphnis. Echo is mentioned in the tale. In any case, the apartment Ray and Chloe inhabit on Vestry Street is a boho Eden, every hipster's wettest dream of Manhattan digs.

The Sunday after reading *Chronicles,* a blustery afternoon in New York, I took a subway to Franklin Street and walked north then west along Vestry, looking for the building that might have housed it. Bob describes it precisely: Federal style, facing a Roman Catholic church with a bell tower, on the same block as the Bull's Head Tavern, below Canal Street, not far from the Hudson River. The neighborhood hasn't changed much since the early sixties, but I could find no structure that resembled it. Not the church, not the Bull's Head Tavern. Houses disappear, but churches aren't often torn down. I wanted to locate that apartment, only because he'd described it so beautifully. Perhaps I missed it.

I also think it telling that the cover photograph of *Chronicles* shows Times Square, the heart and symbol of New York. Didn't he claim, in Shelton's biography, that he had done some Midnight Cowboy hustling there, after first reaching the city? That's an odd juxtaposition to calling home and asking if David had shoveled the walk. In any case, Times Square and the Lou Levy, midtown showbiz side of Manhattan was what reached all of us as teenagers during the 1950s. Live television was there, music publishing and the Brill Building were there, Columbia Records was there. The Ed Sullivan Theater, where he would have seen Elvis sing "Heartbreak Hotel" on television, was there. *Your Hit Parade* was there, broadcast from Radio City in the same studio now used by *Saturday Night Live.* Bob mentions having watched that show, and the vision of the Great White Way that TV pioneers like my uncle launched across the airwaves thrilled kids nationwide. In *Chronicles,* Bob doesn't get to Greenwich Village until his second scene. Times Square held the mystery.

In the folk-music sections, I'm reminded not only of a Greenwich Village I likewise loved, but of the frontier house and outbuildings

Echo at the Hull-Rust Mine Overlook in Hibbing

of Matt and Martha Helstrom, Echo's parents. Matt still had the sound of the old country in his voice, he owned guitars, and he was a rough-and-tumble outdoorsman. Martha Helstrom, as Bob accurately describes her, was "like Mother Earth." The world of their hearth and of those ancient 78s where he first heard Hank

Snow, Jim Reeves, Cowboy Copas, Spade Cooley, Pee Wee King and his Golden West Cowboys, and Eddie Arnold was a world he didn't wish to leave. It was, likewise, Echo's world. Their dream of escaping Hibbing, as kids, was that he would be a singer and she would be a movie star. She told me that on one trip, after his early albums' successes, Bob visited Minneapolis and tried to get her to move back to New York so that they could be together. But he was with Joan Baez and Echo knew that. Possibly he was just drunk— but maybe he didn't wish to relinquish their dream. About that time, and at the end of *Chronicles,* his young character would leave the relative paradise of folk music for the pop satanic mills.

Finally, Toby, how closely do you still follow Dylan's career, including concerts and albums? Do you have a large Dylan archive of official and unofficial recordings? And thirty-four years on from your book, what do you feel about the overall achievement of Bob Dylan?

The last Dylan concert I saw was in 1994, at Manhattan's Roseland ballroom. It's a small venue, and I stood in the mosh pit, perhaps fifteen feet from him. He was smiling, looked relaxed and happy at being in the city. Sheryl Crow had opened for him. He was excellent at first, but his set grew tedious with oldies, that "package of heavy rotting meat," as he calls them, and I left in the middle of "The Times They Are A-Changin'."

I'm keen to see him perform his new material. [I did so in Bozeman, Montana, in July 2005, and in Santiago, Chile, in March 2008.] The musical numbers in *Masked and Anonymous* are iconic. I purchase his new albums the week they appear, and glance at or read thoroughly each new biography. I own all his official recordings, including some early bootlegs. I get through Hibbing every few years and am amused at its attempts to immortalize him, via late May's "Dylan Days." The Chamber of Commerce website has a rather detailed history of Bob and Echo. That must make them laugh. They *are* the town's Tom Sawyer and Becky Thatcher. Zimmy's Downtown Bar and Grill—packed with Dylan memorabilia—is a kick. Last time I was there, whoever owns the Seventh Avenue house had remodeled its interior and given Bob's bedroom window to Zimmy's. It's displayed, frame, sash, and all.

Bob's achievement is large, yet its true size is inestimable. He's a complete and dedicated artist, and no figure speaks more directly for his time. Among his other talents, he's a great singer—the way Louis Armstrong was a great singer. He changed the phrasing of popular singing as thoroughly as Armstrong did. Bob's lyrics are as good as any ever written, and the poetry in them will no doubt move future generations.

His recent *60 Minutes* interview, combined with the revelations in *Chronicles*, enforces the impression many have shared that he is a painfully shy and sensitive individual, one who finds the foot-lights a comfort yet intimacy a chore, and who feels existence in all its nuances more keenly than most of us. On *60 Minutes* he spoke of the bargain he'd made "with the Chief Commander" to keep writing, to keep singing. I'd like to think that bargain is firm. And that he'll persevere.

Toby Thompson is associate professor of English at Penn State University. He is the author of *The Sixties Report* and *Saloon,* and his writing has been published in numerous magazines and newspapers, including *Vanity Fair, Esquire, Rolling Stone,* the *New York Times,* the *Washington Post,* and the *Village Voice.*